Reflections on Glass

20TH CENTURY STAINED GLASS IN AMERICAN ART AND ARCHITECTURE

Reflections on Glass

20TH CENTURY STAINED GLASS IN AMERICAN ART AND ARCHITECTURE

by Virginia Chieffo Raguin

with an essay by Patricia C. Pongracz

The Gallery at the American Bible Society
December 13, 2002 – March 15, 2003

This catalog accompanies the exhibition
Reflections on Glass: Twentieth Century
Stained Glass in American Art and Architecture,
on display from December 13, 2002–March 15, 2003,
at The Gallery at the American Bible Society.

1865 Broadway (at 61st Street)
New York, New York, 10023
www.americanbible.org
Phone 212.408.1500
Fax 212.408.1456

This exhibition was curated by Virginia Raguin and
organized at the American Bible Society by Patricia C. Pongracz.
Catalog published by the American Bible Society.

CATALOG DESIGN Kara Van Woerden
EDITOR Patricia C. Pongracz
CONTRIBUTING EDITOR Mihaela Georgescu
EXHIBITION DESIGN Lou Storey

Printed in the United States by
Toppan Printing Company America, Inc.

Item 112836
ISBN 158516715–0

TABLE OF CONTENTS

ACKNOWLEGMENTS

WHERE TO BEGIN? In reflection, there is an enormous list of people, places and sites that all contributed to this catalog. I owe a great deal to the people I have worked with over many years, especially the parishioners of sites and my colleagues in the International Corpus Vitrearum, many deeply attached to the exploration of cultural heritage of a recent as well as a distant past. Jane Hayward first introduced me to efforts to catalog stained glass since the 1800s in American buildings. American stained glass studios have instructed me, as well as the students I have taught at Holy Cross.

In putting this exhibition together I am most grateful for Dr. Ena Heller's leadership in the Gallery, pioneering exploration of glass in places of worship. My first experience with working with her was the exhibition *Glory in Glass: Stained Glass in the United States, Origins, Variety and Preservation*, on view at The Gallery at the American Bible Society November 12, 1998 through February 16, 1999. Patricia Pongracz, Curator at The Gallery at the American Bible Society, has been a model of the dedicated enthusiast and consummate professional. Her shepherding of all aspects of the catalog and the installation has been guided by her commitment to bringing the public, scholar, and artist into closer communication. Ute Schmid has been a vital part of the conceptualization as well as the implementation of the catalog. Kim Aycox, Gallery Assistant, has pitched in whenever necessary. Lou Storey, our designer, has been highly adaptive to the challenge of this new material. The talent of graphic designer Kara Van Woerden is evident throughout the catalog. Gina Fuentes Walker took many of the photographs reproduced here.

The richness of this exhibition is due in no small part to the many people and institutions who participated in various ways. For all their help with information I thank the Rev. Thomas Kramer, Cathedral of the Holy Spirit, Bismarck, North Dakota; Laura Vernard, All Saints Parish, Brookline, Massachusettes; Nigel Johnson, Cohoes Design; Judi Jordan, Richard and Katie Goss, *Stained Glass Magazine*; Barea Lamb Seeley; Helene Weis; Edith Gilsoul; Jerry Cobb, S. J., Ph. D., Seattle University; Dr. Ivo Rauch, Koblenz, Germany; Gail Tierney; Ulricke Brinckman, Cathedral Supervision, Cologne, Germany; Mark Liebowitz, Wilmark Studios; Carol Frenning; Carol Newman de Vegvar, Ohio Wesleyan University; Gordon Huether, Architectural Glass Design; Jean Farnsworth; Dr. Robert Brill, The Corning Museum of Glass; Beth Hylen, The Rakow Library, Corning Museum of Glass as well as the libraries of the College of the Holy Cross, Tufts University; Harvard University, Fine Arts Library; Loeb Library of the School of Art and Design, Harvard University; and the Boston Public Library. A portion of expenses of research was supported by the Research and Publications Fund, The College of the Holy Cross.

I am grateful to the artists represented in the catalog who offered images and information on their various commissions: Robert Pinart, Ed Carpenter, James Carpenter, Arthur Stern, Mark Eric Gulsrud, Hendrik Van de Burgt, Albinas Elskus, Helen Carew Hickman, Charles Z. Lawrence, Robert Kehlmann, Saara Gallin, Mary Clerkin Higgins, Sylvia Nicolas, J. Kenneth Leap, and David Frasier.

To the contemporary glass artists highlighted in the exhibition I owe a special debt of gratitude: Steven Holl, Douglas Hansen, Stephen Knapp, Linda Lichtman, Ellen Mandelbaum, Ellen Miret and David Wilson. Their enthusiasm and generosity made our collaboration a memorable one.

Many people aided in the smooth implementation of the exhibition. I am grateful to those institutions and individuals who loaned works and were generous in providing information about them: Dr. Tina Oldknow, Curator, 20th Century Glass, Corning Museum of Glass; Janice Chadbourne, Boston Public Library; Peter A. Rohlf, Rohlf's Stained and Leaded Glass Studio, Inc.; Donald Samick, Lamb Studios; John Salisbury, Gaytee Stained Glass; Gary L. Helf, Franklin Art Glass Studios; Bernard Gruenke, Senior, Bernard Gruenke, Junior, Gunar Gruenke, and Patricia Zimmerman, Conrad Schmitt Studios; Derix Glasstudios, Taunusstein, Germany; Gabriel Mayer, Munich, Germany; Terry Blaine; Michael Cullinane, Judith O'Connell, of Bendheim; David Wagner; Dan Waber, Richard Elliot, and Doug Little, Kokomo Opalescent Glass; Ward and Lorna Lovells, Uroboros Glass Studios, Inc.

Lastly, I cite my continuing debt to my family, especially my husband Michel, and my two sons, Daniel and John, who have accompanied me on innumerable excursions – "show Mom a building and she's happy." I dedicate this effort to Rachel, Katherine, Chantal, and Eric.

PRESIDENT'S PREFACE

IN NOVEMBER 1998, The Gallery at the American Bible Society organized an exhibition entitled *Glory in Glass: Stained Glass in the United States. Origins, Variety, and Preservation*. Under the direction of Prof. Virginia C. Raguin, the exhibition chronicled stained glass designed for religious buildings in the nineteenth and early twentieth centuries in the United States. The exhibition, which was extremely well received, started a dialogue about the function and symbolism of stained glass in the context of places of worship. That dialogue is now continued in *Reflections on Glass: Twentieth Century Stained Glass in American Art and Architecture*, a uniquely diverse and comprehensive display of both traditional stained glass and cutting-edge work by modern interpreters of this medieval art form.

The art of stained glass, whose historical significance is intrinsically linked to the symbolism of light, is particularly well-matched to the mission of our Gallery. Light has long been recognized as a uniquely suited metaphor for the divine. The Bible tells us "God is light, and there is no darkness at all in him" (John 1.5). This inherent spiritual quality makes light assume a particularly important role in the architecture of places of worship and the art connected with liturgy and ritual.

Church windows decorated with stained glass are an apt visual metaphor for Christ's light. Light passes through the colored glass and is transformed into reflected and refracted colored rays. The window glows and casts jeweled rays, bathing the interior with diffuse, colored light. As light permeates the material world around us, it becomes a symbol of spiritual and intellectual growth: learning is enlightenment. "Teaching gives light and brings wisdom to the ignorant" (Psalm 119.130). We hope that you will learn something from this exhibition, while you enjoy its radiance.

Eugene B. Habecker, Ph.D.
President, American Bible Society

INTRODUCTION

REFLECTIONS ON GLASS: *Twentieth Century Stained Glass in American Art and Architecture* examines stained glass windows in light of twentieth century sacred architectural aesthetics, as well as in the context of the community for which they were created. The exhibition chronicles the complex and diverse development of stained glass as an architectural art over the course of the twentieth century and into the twenty first. The catalog, divided into chapters on the basis of style, attempts to place the choice of style in its historical context. Chapter 1 shows how twentieth-century stained glass developed out of the ideals fueling the nineteenth century's Gothic Revival. Chapters 2, 3 and 4 illustrate the changes in stained glass over the course of the century from opalescent pictorialism, to the architectural styles of Arts and Crafts, Art Nouveau, Art Deco and back again to Gothic Revival. These chapters illustrate how and when these changes occurred and show that often many styles were favored simultaneously, emphasizing that stained glass did not follow any strict linear progression of style. Chapter 5 illustrates the profound influence that international artists had on American stained glass of the twentieth century. The 17 major artists profiled were, and in many cases continue to be, sensitive to artistic changes abroad and their work reflects the international context out of which it was borne. Chapter 6 traces the technical history of the medium showing the numerous innovations in stained glass technique employed over the twentieth century and their reliance on the medium's technical tradition.

As much as all art is dependent on the integrity and skill of the artist, the direction of that artist's expression is linked to circumstances of exposure, inspiration and, especially in architecture and its allied arts, to the client. This exhibition focuses on the artistic issues of the craft and above all on changes in style. Stained glass's continuing development is embodied by the seven focus artists at the heart of the exhibition: Douglas Hansen, Steven Holl, Stephen Knapp, Linda Lichtman, Ellen Mandelbaum, Ellen Miret, and David Wilson – all of whom demonstrate the importance of stained glass in an architectural context. They are profiled in Chapter 7, each explaining a significant, recent architectural commission.

The goal of the exhibition is to emphasize works on glass as destined for architectural space while providing the viewer with a more intimate acquaintance with the design process of this most architectural art. In the process we hope to illustrate that art is not made by a single individual, but by the intersection of individuals: the community who define what they need from a building, the suppliers of quality architectural materials, the designers and craftspeople executing the building and its windows and the subsequent users of the space.

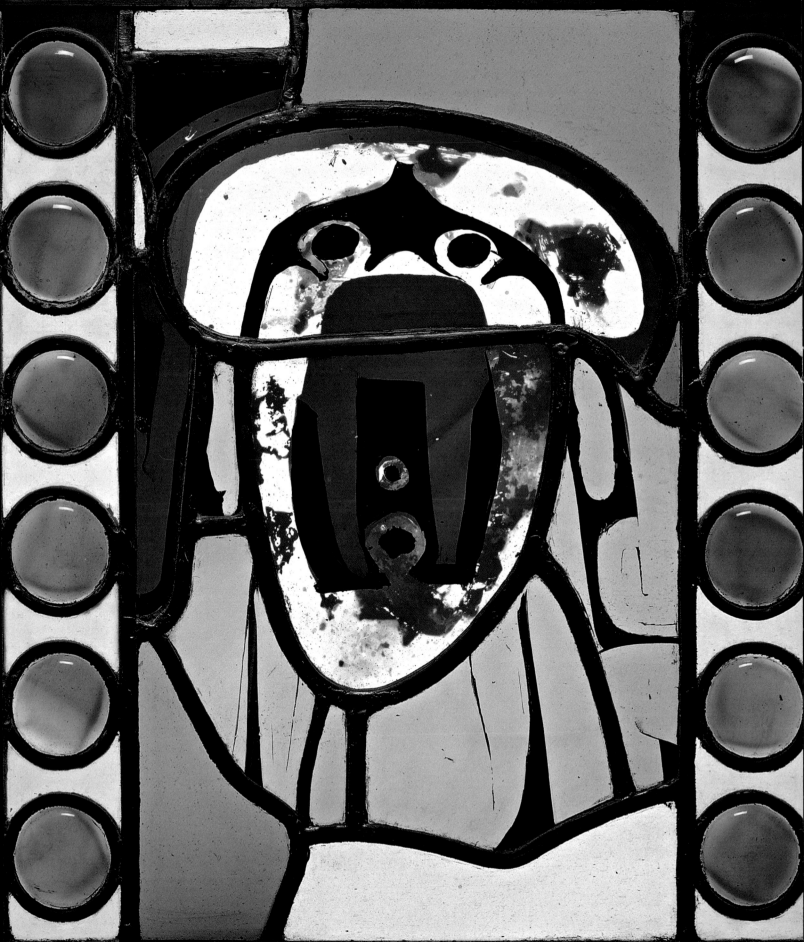

I STAINED GLASS CONSIDERED: A PAST CENTURY AND TODAY

Where will the arts meet again to reinforce one another as they have done in the great epochs of the past?

Robert Sowers, *The Lost Art*, 1954[1]

Is stained glass a branch of the fine arts – or is it a craft? In the creation and appreciation of the window, do we find principles of the art that underlie all great works in glass from the Middle Ages to the present?[2] For houses of worship, is there an ideal style – or even shape – of building that offers a perfect setting for performance of a specific kind of worship? In designing for sacred spaces, does the stained glass artist create autonomously or does he or she simply conform to the dictates of the architect? Who writes about stained glass, and with what authority? These questions have animated the discussion of stained glass since its nineteenth-century revival and the development of our modern forms of collecting art through galleries and museums. Today, as we enter the twenty-first century, we can add another vital question – that of the image in art. What is the function of the recognizable, "teaching" image for faith communities? In painting, sculpture, and glass, can we identify imagery understood by communities of believers to express their deeply-held spiritual aspirations that can be used by an artist?

Nineteenth-century proponents of the architectural style known as the Gothic Revival sought to recapture what they saw as the purity of thought, architectural form and religion in the Middle Ages. Far from being a dry academic exercise, the Neo-Gothic style was deeply intertwined with a revival of "sensible" religion – a search for ritual forms and buildings that touched the soul and brought the individual into intimation of the divine. As a wide range of stained glass artists with highly divergent styles attest, the glass of the Middle Ages offered compelling examples and rich models to emulate. For example, Charles J. Connick (1875–1945), designer of the medieval inspired *Coronation of the Virgin* of the 1920s (figure 1), Robert Sowers (1923–1990), designer of a Modernist panel from 1952 (figure 2), and Albinas Elskus (1926–) arguably the major proponent of realist imagery and meticulous draftsmanship in the last third of the twentieth century (figure 3), all speak of being profoundly influenced by Gothic architecture (figure 4) and stained glass windows (figure 5) exemplified for them by the cathedral of Chartres.[3] The following essay traces the aesthetic development of stained glass and its critical reception in the United States beginning in the nineteenth century. Given the constant reference to glass of the Middle Ages by critics and artists alike, we begin by exploring medieval stained glass and the society that produced it.

The Middle Ages
The medieval designer produced both the iconic (image rich) and aniconic (image absent) window. Within each church, sculpted or painted images enunciated the creed of the makers while designating the hierarchy of space.[4] Windows also organized the interior, filling the entire space with light and form (figure 6). In the ideal building campaign, great window programs were conceived and most

FIGURE 1
Charles J. Connick (1875–1945)

Coronation of the Virgin (detail), late 1920s

Boston Public Library, Boston, MA

FIGURE 2
Robert Sowers (1923–1990)

Red One (detail), 1952

The Corning Museum of Glass, Corning, NY

FIGURE 3
Albinas Elskus (1926–)

Three Marys at the Tomb (detail), 1985

Mausoleum of the Good Shepherd, St. Gertrude's Cemetery, Colonia, NJ

often underway as the building itself was nearing completion. The art historian Madeline Caviness describes the reuse and alteration of cartoons (full-scale line designs on wood, vellum, or linen for stained glass windows) in the twelfth-century glazing of the choir of Saint-Remi, Reims, even as the architecture was in the final stages of construction: "the sequence suggested here shows artists designing in series, each modification based on a critique of completed panels viewed in their intended position in the building."[5] In short, windows were designed as part of the architectural ensemble, not as an added embellishment to merely decorate the building.

Architects, designers and glaziers alike considered how window placement would affect the architecture, as well as how windows would illuminate yet be seen within their architectural setting. These considerations guided decisions regarding the placement of both figural (with their selected narrative structures) and non-figural windows. For example, an image of the *Crucifixion* or the *Passion of Christ* would often be placed behind the main altar in the east end of a church. The colored glass narrative linked the ritual action taking place beneath it, the consecration of the Eucharist, to the action that precipitated it: Jesus's suffering and death that led to the salvation of his earthbound faithful. Considerations regarding the place of stained glass windows in architecture, their effect on the space and their perception by a varied audience, composed of lay faithful and ecclesiastics alike, are as active today as they were when Gothic was born.

The distinguishing feature of the Middle Ages in the West was that society shared a belief in the same Christian rituals and forms (including images) that communicated both social and religious meaning. In most regions, church and state were linked to one another and populations were ethnically monolithic. Europe shared a single common base of biblical text and saints' legends (with some local variation). To the medieval mind, art and ritual were a way to transcend time and place, to tap into the universal truths offered by the divine. Despite broad thematic unity, however, no two artistic statements were ever exactly alike. For example, the birth of Christ was an expected presence on a

FIGURE 4
West Façade
Cathedral of Chartres,
1140–1220
Chartres, France

FIGURE 5
Jesse Tree Window,
1145–55
Cathedral of Chartres
Chartres, France

FIGURE 6
**View into the first bay
of the north transept**
**Cathedral of Auxerre,
c. 1280**
Auxerre, France

Gothic sculptured portal and each element of the story, the infant in the manger, the shepherds, the magi, and King Herod, was easily recognizable. Their placement in any given artistic interpretation, however, differed to construct and express meaning particularly relevant to the local audience. For example, at the cathedral of Notre Dame in Paris, within walking distance of the royal residence, the west portal sculpture emphasizes the three kings, carving in stone the belief that a divinely inspired monarch ruled France. All art of the time, be it manuscripts, wall painting, sculpture or metalwork, employed similar systems of framed and interrelated images. Emphasizing the power of these "seen" truths, that informed and reinforced the belief system, was the fact that the vast majority of people saw images only in church. Not until Johannes Gutenberg's (c. 1397–1468) invention of the printing press in the 1450s and the mechanical reproduction of images it heralded were images available to a broader, though still limited, audience for use in their own homes.

Medieval Christian art in Europe presupposed a shared culture among the maker, the patron and viewers. In this system, an artist was perceived as an agent expressing visually the culture's beliefs. Thus judgments of quality focused primarily on the evaluation of the usefulness of the artist's work, not on the artist himself. Most art made during the Middle Ages is, after all, unsigned. Abbot Suger (1081–1155) of Saint-Denis, a royal Benedictine monastery founded in the seventh century in Paris, articulated criteria for judging art in his *Book of Suger Abbot of St. Denis on What Was Done During his Administration* (c. 1144–1148).[6] Suger believed that the importance of the object's use was reflected both by the value of the materials used, and the creator's skill in manipulating them. The significance of the object for Suger was its ability to offer a locus of transcendence for the viewer:

Thus sometimes when, because of my delight in the beauty of the house of God, the multicolor loveliness of the gems has called me away from external cares, and worthy meditation, transporting me from material to immaterial things, has persuaded me to examine the diversity of holy virtues, then I seem to see myself existing on some level, as it were, beyond our earthly one, neither completely the slime of the earth nor completely in the purity of heaven. By the gift of God I can be transported in an anagogical manner from this inferior level to that superior one.[7]

Windows were made of glass, iron, and lead, considered costly materials in the Middle Ages; indeed their value was frequently described in terms of precious stones. Suger's text suggests many analogies.[8] Windows were essential to the fabric of a church for the medieval thinker and viewer. Their colored glass modulated light within the interior space while illustrating the sacred narrative that defined the faith. Images and scenes leaded together into windows literally and symbolically shed light on the central drama of salvation, enacted daily in the ritual consecration of the Eucharist during Mass, when Christ's sacrifice became present to worshipers.

Nineteenth-Century Perceptions of Historic Windows and the Revival of Stained Glass

The nineteenth century, unlike the Middle Ages, was a literate society, and proponents of ideas invariably communicated through the printed word, a practice that continues today.[9] It also was a heterogeneous one, with many different traditions vying for acceptance. With the revival of stained glass, artists, no longer anonymous, wrote about stained glass windows from their personal perspectives. These practitioners looked back at a long history of stained glass and attempted to qualify the specific styles most worthy of emulation in the revival. For example, William Warrington (1796–1869) advocated the English Perpendicular

Gothic of the fourteenth and fifteenth centuries.[10] He published at his own expense a lavish folio volume entitled *History of Stained Glass from the Earliest Period of the Art to the Present Time*.[11] Although the text is described in the subtitle as being *Illustrated by coloured examples of entire windows in the various styles*, all the examples are taken from Warrington's own designs. The author explains this decision:

It is *necessary* to improve public taste or the art itself can never be generally improved. But it is by the production of good *modern* works that this must principally be effected. Hence the Author has chosen to give a series of his own designs... composed on the most rigid principles of ancient art.[12]

Among the most influential writers was Charles Winston (1814–65), a lawyer and also a designer of windows.[13] He illustrated his publications with watercolors of important medieval windows, defining the characteristics of English period styles.[14] Winston published in 1847 a survey known by its short title of *Hints on Glasspainting* and collected papers, *Memoirs Illustrative of the Art of Glass-Painting*, posthumously. In it he achieved a remarkably even-handed evaluation of the characteristics of English period styles[15] (figures 7, 8). Winston was personally convinced of the superiority of early sixteenth-century glass painting, in a full-blown Renaissance style with three-dimensional modeling, and yet his publications meticulously analyzed all styles.

Catalogs by commercial studios also included information about glass production and historic styles that could be produced for the client. For example, the studios Heaton, Butler & Bayne (1855–1953?),[16] London, and the Chance Brothers of Birmingham, England issued sale catalogs illustrating their firms' work which included critical commentary on the aesthetics of stained glass.[17] Although

they also made statements on the superiority of glass produced in one historic style over another, they advertised their ability to work in all styles.

The writing by the studios reflected the contemporary architectural polemic. Beginning in the nineteenth century, architects argued that specific styles of architecture were suited to specific types of human activities – for example, classical style for a bank, Gothic for a church. Proponents of the Gothic Revival believed that architectural style had the capacity to effect, or reflect, the moral qualities of the actions they housed.[18] The English architect Augustus W. N. Pugin (1812–1852) wrote *Contrasts, or a Parallel between the Noble Edifices of the Middle Ages and Corresponding Buildings Showing the Present Decay of Taste*[19] in which he argued that both religion and social values may be invigorated through a rebirth of the Gothic style.[20] Pugin's interest extended beyond the building to stained glass, wall coverings, tiles, furniture, and ecclesiastic vessels, such at those he published in *The Glossary of Ecclesiastic Ornament and Costume*.[21]

French architect Eugène Viollet-le-Duc (1814–1879) restored many medieval buildings including the Cathedral of Notre-Dame of Paris in 1843 and the twelfth-century Abbey of Vézelay, in Burgundy in 1847 both considered paragons of medieval architecture.[22] Viollet-le-Duc's writing on architecture culminated in his multi-volume *Dictionnaire raisonné de l'architecture française du XIe au XVIe siècle*, 1854–68.[23] Volume nine contains an article on stained glass entitled *Vitrail*, which describes and illustrates notable examples of medieval stained glass windows. *Vitrail* enjoyed enormous influence on the craft of stained glass. It was published in numerous translations, and illustrations were borrowed liberally by other writers, such as Nathaniel Hubert John Westlake (1833–1921).

Westlake became known in the United States through his work and his writing. He made a number of windows for American churches, including a

FIGURE 7

**Charles Winston
(1814–1856)**

Drawings of:

**Merton College Chapel,
Oxford, c. 1300**

**Lincoln Cathedral,
c. 1300**

FIGURE 8

**Charles Winston
(1814-1856)**

**Grisailles of Salisbury
Cathedral, 1265–70**

large chancel window in Trinity Church, New Orleans, Louisiana; windows in Gate of Heaven Church, Boston, and those in the Carroll Centre, Newton, Massachusetts.[24] Westlake wrote *A History of Design in Stained and Painted Glass*, a four-volume history of the medium.[25] The illustrations in his volumes were of such high quality that they were frequently used as cartoons for windows: many twentieth-century studios would score Westlake's illustrations in a grid in order to enlarge them directly onto glass (figure 9).

The long-standing belief that there are unique and definable true principles of glass design encouraged American practitioners to follow their European colleagues and write about their own experiences with the medium in treatises, pamphlets and books. The work of Otto Heinigke (1850–1915?) and Harry Eldredge Goodhue (1873–1918), discussed in Chapter 3, remains some of the most insightful and important. *The National Ornamental Glass Manufacturers Association* founded in 1903, in part as a means of confronting foreign competition and lobbying for duties on imported windows, provided a forum for American glass painters to share their thoughts on the medium. With the publication of *The Ornamental Glass Bulletin* beginning in 1906, edited by Joseph E. Flanagan (1858–1928) from 1906 through 1928, the association played a central role in the dissemination of practitioner's writing as well as critiques of contemporary glass production. The organization, now know as the *Stained Glass Association of America* (SGAA), continues to play a pivotal role in the field, publishing a quarterly magazine called *Stained Glass* with articles on criticism and history.[26]

Orin E. Skinner (1892–1995) and Charles J. Connick of the Connick Studio, Boston, Massachusetts, discussed in Chapter 4, were early advocates for the study of historic windows in American collections. Skinner's tenure from 1933 to 1948 as editor of *Stained Glass* was particularly important. In an effort to understand their role in the continuing tradition of stained glass windows, they surveyed historic glass panels in museum collections, as well as installations of modern glass in American cities, field work chronicled in *Stained Glass*. Skinner and Connick also were interested in the influences of the work of their colleagues abroad. To that end, they published commissioned articles by European glass painters on historic windows in their own cities. In 1937, Connick published *Adventures in Light and Color*,[27] a deeply felt reflection on his fascination with stained glass as an art and his own creative impetus (figure 10). In it, Connick's own work is indivisible from the historic windows he so admired.

Robert Sowers was admired as both a practitioner and a theorist. A catalyst for bringing the Modern German school to the attention of American artists, discussed in Chapter 5. Sowers was awarded a Fulbright Fellowship in 1950 for travel to Europe, primarily England. He entered into an established glass writing tradition when he published *The Lost Art* in 1954.[28] He subtitled it *A survey of one thousand years of stained glass* and asked Sir Herbert Read, the distinguished art historian and museum curator, to write an introduction, perhaps in an effort to secure validation for his field from the academy. Read had written his own work on stained glass in 1926 entitled *English Stained Glass*.[29] Sowers devoted about twenty pages to historic periods, and about fifty pages to contemporary glass. He interspersed his prose with selective comparisons with medieval examples to define what he saw as issues of architecture and light. Despite its brevity, *The Lost Art* is a comprehensive call for the "rediscovery of plastic essentials"[30] and for the collaborative work of designing wall treatment as a vital part of an architectural ensemble. Sowers's own work, such as the American Airlines Terminal at Kennedy International Airport, New York, 1959, testifies to his principles.

PLATE LXI.—*a*, SUBJECT FROM THE LIFE OF S. PETER, AND VOTIVE FIGURE, FROM BEAUVAIS CATHEDRAL; *b*, DETAILS OF THE CANOPY OVER THE SUBJECT *a*, AS THEY SHOULD HAVE BEEN DRAWN IN PL. *a*.

FIGURE 9

**Nathaniel Westlake
(1833–1921)**

**Life of Thomas and
detail of a canopy**

Beauvais Cathedral,
c. 1300

Beauvais, France

From *Vitrail*

FIGURE 10

Eugène Viollet-le-Duc (1814–1879)

Seated King from Jesse Tree of Chartres Cathedral, c. 1145–55

After *Dictionnnaire raisonné de l'architecture française*, 1854–68

Reprinted by Charles Connick, *Adventures in Light and Color*, 1937

The tradition of glass painters and makers writing about their art continues today. Recent writing on glass includes Brian Clarke's (1953–) *Architectural Stained Glass*,[31] produced in collaboration with other stained glass artists. The work is notable for its trenchant essays concerning artistic principles, as well as its profiles of major designers. Andrew Moor (1946–), a glass art consultant, has produced two important books, *Contemporary Stained Glass* (1989) and most recently, *Architectural Glass Art* (1997).[32] Moor's books give an international survey of the field. Although focusing on secular contexts, the books' organization around thematic concepts brings coherence to the discussion of artistic work that has equal viability in religious expression.

The Twentieth Century, the Image, and the Position of Stained Glass

The role that stained glass played in the Gothic revival of the nineteenth century was similar in many ways to its function in the Gothic period of the Middle Ages. In both the thirteenth and nineteenth centuries glass was perceived as a public, architectural art. Architects worked with glass artists to design architectural space. In both periods, society shared a general familiarity with stories drawn from the Bible. It provided a wealth of images, both narrative and individual figures, instantly recognizable to many viewers. Church glass that illustrated biblical stories or made reference to the Christian narrative could presume some level of understanding by the viewer.

Attitudes towards figural art that developed during the Modern period (1930s–1980s) changed the role of the image, profoundly altering church architecture and with it, the value of stained glass. The very definition of art would become more restrictive and highly prejudicial for the practitioner of architectural glass. Art would be defined as primarily an aesthetic experience, purified from any practical demands. The artist became viewed as someone separate from his or her society, actually ill at ease when his or her work did not "challenge" prevailing concepts. Modern design in practical work, such as furniture, still could be tastefully executed, but had become relegated to the status of "decorative arts."

The Modern period, however, did have a spiritual agenda – a search for universals, basic forms that would strike deep chords in a broad spectrum of viewers.[33] It made a moral commitment to transcend cultural barriers – for it was born, in part, out of the time of two world wars, when artists were sensitive to the fact that artistic styles had been appropriated to signify national identities and destructive political agendas. For example, under the direction of Albert Speer (1905–1981), the Third Reich built monumental state architecture in a traditional classical style linking itself visually with the traditions of other great ancient states of Greece and Rome. With such examples fresh in the minds of artists, architects, and visual designers, their unified move away from explicit subject matter or historic styles is not surprising.

Proponents of the Modern Art movement believed that by striking down resonances with the past, art could support a climate where the elemental unity of humankind could be acknowledged. Art of the past was still valued, but discussion of it and comparison among styles shifted to a search for shared formal principles. Artists wanted to demonstrate that basic principles of form appear equally in a Japanese print, an African Mask, Pablo Picasso's abstractions, or Mies von der Rohe's *Barcelona Pavilion* – that universal formal principles existed that transcended time, culture, and place. Sowers, for example, brilliantly argued the similarities of a detail of the water carriers from the Mary Magdalene window at Chartres cathedral (1215–20) to Picasso's *Girl before a Mirror* (1932).[34] Sowers, however, so in touch with the monumental tradition, found that:

although it is an exceptional painting by current standards, [it] makes allusions to stained glass which seem false and contrived in the presence of a fragment from Chartres. Picasso commands here neither the scale nor the conviction of the traditional artisan whose image bespeaks the accumulated wisdom of untold generations.[35]

Sowers also addressed the changes religious art underwent in the twentieth century, writing that "in the catacombs there was an image without art: are we now to have art without image?"[36] At the height of the Modern Art movement, he questioned the effect of a non-figural aesthetic on contemporary religious art, wondering how society "deal[s] with religious themes in an age when art is almost totally secular and private in character?"[37] Sowers was keenly aware of the issue of use, practicality, and service of art to the broad needs of society, and the contemporary relegation of art to aesthetic pleasure. He decried:

the poverty of imagery that extends across the world like a great drought. The Never-never land between the decorative and the symbolic has now become the battlefield on which the artist must cry for a *place*, literally, in our environment – where art can gain that meaning which it only has when celebrating vital human activities.[38]

How does art celebrate vital human activities as argued by Sowers? An artist who has retained the recognizable image and contemporary concerns within Modernism is the American Robert Rauschenberg (1925–). His paintings have explored pictorial space and memory, expressive use of color, and painterly and illustrative image. Rauschenberg spoke of conceiving the picture plane as a flatbed on which to build works that would bridge the gulf between abstraction and representation.[39] His *Retroactive 1* (figure 11) features at its center a picture of John F. Kennedy. He points his index finger in a demonstrative gesture, emphasized by the repeated image of his hand to the left, that many will associate with his inaugural challenge, "Ask not what your country can do for you, ask what you can do for your country." Other images include an astronaut floating in space, upper left, and fragments of a Renaissance painting, lower right, making a connection between the historic nude, vulnerable figure and the contemporary human body isolated in outer space. Rauschenberg combines these snapshots in an attempt to emphasize the complex nature of our collected memories and to demonstrate that the call for human courage extends across time and societies. We find, even in Modernist language, that works can incorporate an "iconography" – a sequence of images that narrate a belief system. Is this not a model for interaction in glass?

Post Modern Architecture and the Role of Stained Glass

Since stained glass is inextricably linked to architecture, changes in architectural practice condition the direction of the field. Because of the altered role of religion in contemporary American life, church architecture and stained glass, in particular, have not developed apace with secular buildings. The situation forms a sharp contrast to a survey of progressive architects a little over a century ago when architectural firms such as Henry Hobson Richardson (1838–86), with Trinity Church in Boston; Leopold Eidlitz (1823–1908), with Temple Emanu-El, New York (demolished 1928); and James Renwick (1818–95), with St Patrick's Cathedral, New York, were distinguished by the number of churches and synagogues they designed. In contrast, today religious architecture is not well represented in most overviews of new building. For example, in Charles Jenks's *Architecture Today*, out of 541 images, only seven relate to churches.[40] Stained

FIGURE 11

**Robert Rauschenberg
(1925–)**

Retroactive I, **1964**

Oil and silkscreened ink
on canvas

Wadsworth Atheneum,
Hartford, CT

glass design follows these trends. Secular stained glass installations have vastly increased, as evident in Andrew Moor's *Contemporary Stained Glass* which profiled over sixty artists working in a secular context. *Architectural Glass Art*, published in 1997, included stained glass made for houses of worship, but still the preponderance of progressive examples are windows for museums, airports, medical centers, shopping malls, corporate head-quarters, and residences.

As we move into the twenty-first century, we see architecture that is more flexible and attuned to sensuality and even overt symbolism. Whereas Modern architecture advocated a single "international" or "non style" style, Post Modern architecture, that saw its beginnings in the 1980s, is far more varied in expression and accepting of a wider variety of shapes and materials. Contemporary architecture is often deliberately eclectic. For example, Philip Johnson's AT&T Building, New York City (figure 12) makes a clear directional turn from the understated glass and steel modernity of Mies van der Rohe's Seagram Building (1954–1958), New York City (figure 13). The AT&T Building, an iconic example of Post Modern architecture, is a Modern skyscraper made of pink granite. Its base, enclosing a public plaza, features a monumental portal program. A central towering arched portal is flanked by three rectangular doorways on each side. The building's shaft has nine stripes of vertical fenestration reminiscent of a Rolls Royce's radiator grill. The building is capped by a split pediment – alluding to Chippendale highboys. The eclectic architecture evokes Romanesque and Renaissance precedents while simultaneously incorporating design elements from the earliest skyscrapers.

Stephen Holl's Ignatius Chapel of Seattle University, 1996 (figure 14), uses glass in new ways. The building is heralded for its sensuality of form and embodiment of light as presence, both inside and outside the building. Surely the incorporation

of image, structural element, and beauty, so eloquently demonstrated in architectural glass of the past will find new and vital opportunities in the future.

Religious congregations may very well see a renewal of interest in ritual and in explicit imagery. Many Roman Catholic congregations are already immersed in a reaction to what many term the "iconoclastic" excesses presented as a response to the goals of the Second Vatican Council to bring the church closer to the needs of modern life. The publication in 1978 of *Environment and Art in Catholic Worship* set the tone for American changes. The U. S. Conference of Catholic Bishops issued *Built of Living Stones* on November 16, 2000, urging support of contemporary art that enhances the function of the church as a place of prayer and instruction. Can architectural stained glass studios work more with illustrators, as the growing trend of out-of house-designers appears to suggest? One wonders if this century will see some kind of a contemporary image-bank that will aid artists in their service to adapted to aiding narrative of belief systems and advocacy for charitable works. This exhibition attempts to further that process by reviewing our recent past and displaying the artistic possibilities of the present.

FIGURE 14
Steven Holl Architects
Ignatius Chapel (view of exterior from pool), 1996
Seattle University,
Seattle, WA

ENDNOTES

1 Robert Sowers, *The Lost Art: A Thousand Years of Stained Glass. With an introduction by Sir Herbert Read* (New York, 1954), 60.

2 For a brief but excellent survey see Sarah Brown, *Stained Glass: An Illustrated History* (New York, 1992). A more restricted survey is James L. Sturm, *Stained Glass from Medieval Times to the Present: Treasures to be Seen in New York* (New York, 1982).

3 Charles J. Connick, *Adventures in Light and Color* (New York, 1937), references throughout the text; Robert Sowers, *The Lost Art*, esp. 63-65; Sarah Brown, "Albinas Elskus, an American Master," *The Journal of Stained Glass* 20/1 (1996), 59, speaking of his four days at Chartres.

4 For an overall view of medieval windows see Richard Marks, *Stained Glass in England during the Middle Ages* (Toronto, 1993). The International *Corpus Vitrearum Medii Aevi* (CVMA), an international research group, organized since the late 1940s, has published sixty-eight volumes of stained glass before 1700. Works on Germany, France, England, and the Lowlands are the most numerous but virtually all European countries are represented. Publication of historic glass in United States collections include a complete survey: Madeline H. Caviness and Jane Hayward, ed., *Stained Glass before 1700 in American Collections: Corpus Vitrearum Checklists* I-IV, (Studies in the History of Art, 15, 23, 28, 39) (Washington DC, 1985, 1987, 1989, 1991). Full catalogs have begun with Virginia Raguin/Helen Zakin, *Stained Glass before 1700 in the Collections of the Midwest States, Corpus Vitrearum, United States of America*, VIII/2 (London, 2001). Volumes for the Metropolitan Museum of Art, The Cloisters Collection, are on press.

5 Madeline Caviness, *Sumptuous Arts at the Royal Abbeys in Reims and Braine: Ornatus Elegantiae, Varietate Stupendes* (Princeton, 1990), 107–17, quote on 116.

6 For translations of Suger's work see Erwin Panofsky, *Abbot Suger on the Abbey Church of St.-Denis and its Art Treasures* (Princeton, 1946); second edition, Erwin Panofsky/Gerda Panofsky-Soergel, ed. (Princeton 1979).

7 Ibid., 63–65.

8 Suger refers to "sapphire glass," ibid., 77 and explains that during the consecration, "Certain persons also (deposited) gems out of love and reverence for Jesus Christ, chanting: 'Lapides preciosi mones muri tui,'" Ibid., 102–3. Panofsky identifies the text as appearing in the Roman Breviary, *Commune Dedicationes Ecclesia*, 5th antiphon, that continues "et turres Jerusalem gemmis aedificabuntur" (and the towers of Jerusalem shall be built of gems).

9 Virginia Raguin, "Antiquarianism, Publication and Revival: Stained Glass in the Nineteenth Century," in Virginia Raguin/Mary Ann Powers, *Sacred Spaces: Building and Remembering Sites of Worship in the Nineteenth Century*, exh. cat., Iris & B. Gerald Cantor Art Gallery, College of the Holy Cross (Worcester, 2002), 27–46.

10 Martin Harrison, *Victorian Stained Glass* (London, 1980), 17–18, 84, pl. 2(a); Stanley A. Shepherd in: Paul Atterbury/Clive Wainwright, eds., *Pugin: A Gothic Passion* (New Haven, 1994), 195–206, pl. 380.

11 William Warrington, *History of Stained Glass from the Earliest Period of the Art to the Present Time* (London, 1848).

12 Ibid., unpaginated introduction.

13 One example of his designs is the west window of the church of St. Mary, Bushbury, Staffordshire, England dated 1853, fabricated by Ward & Hughes.

14 J. B. Waring, *Catalogue of Drawings from Ancient Glass Paintings by the Late Charles Winston Esq. of the Inner Temple*, exh. cat., The Arundel Society (London, 1865).

15 Charles Winston, *An Inquiry into the Difference of Style Observable in Ancient Glass Paintings, especially in England: with Hints on Glass Painting, by an Amateur* (Oxford, 1847), id., *Memoirs Illustrative of the Art of Glass Painting* (London, 1865).

16 Clement Heaton (1824–1882); James Butler (1830–1913); Robert Bayne (1837–1915), S. M. B. Bayne, *Heaton, Butler & Bayne, A Hundred Years of the Art of Stained Glass* (Lausanne, 1986). Products of these studios reached all areas of the English-speaking world, see Beverley Sherry, *Australia's Historic Stained Glass* (Sydney, 1991).

17 Heaton and Butler, *Illustrated Catalogue of Stained Glass Windows* (London, 1864); Chance Brothers & Co, *Church Windows: A Series of Designs Original or Selected from Ancient Examples by Sebastian Evans*, M.A. (Birmingham, 1862). See Victoria and Albert Museum, London.

18 David Watkin, *Morality and Architecture: The Development of a Theme in Architectural History and Theory from the Gothic Revival to the Modern Movement* (Oxford, 1977).

19 Augustus W. N. Pugin, *Contrasts, or a Parallel between the Noble Edifices of the Middle Ages and Corresponding Buildings Showing the Present Decay of Taste* (Leicester, 1969).

20 Paul Atterbury, ed., *A. W. N. Pugin: Master of Gothic Revival*, exh. cat., The Bard Center for Studies in the Decorative Arts (New Haven, 1995), and Paul Atterbury and Clive Wainwright, *Pugin: A Gothic Passion*, (New Haven, 1994).

21 Augustus W. N. Pugin, *The Glossary of Ecclesiastic Ornament and Costume* (London, 1844).

22 For both projects see *Viollet-le-Duc; L'éclectisme raisonné* (Paris, 1984), 145–59; Kevin D. Murphy, *Memory and Modernity: Viollet-le-Duc at Vézelay* (University Park, 2000).

23 John Summerson, *Violet-le-Duc*, exh. cat., Grand Palais (Paris, 1980), 395–404, list of Viollet-le-Duc's writings.

24 The Carroll Centre is in a realistic Renaissance style. The window is signed: "Lavers, Westlake & Barraud, London 1882." For discussion of the firm see Harrison, *Victorian Stained Glass*, 33–34, 49–50, 80–81.

25 Nathaniel Hubert John Westlake, *A History of Design in Painted Glass*, 4 vols. (London, 1881–94).

26 Orin Skinner et al., "Mostly About the Magazine," *Stained Glass* 73 (Spring 1978), 13–17.

27 Charles J. Connick, *Adventures in Light and Color* (New York, 1937).

28 Robert Sowers, *The Lost Art: A Survey of One Thousand Years of Stained Glass* (London, 1954).

29 Sir Herbert Read, *English Stained Glass* (London, 1926).

30 Sowers, *The Lost Art*, Chapter 7, 37–39

31 Brian Clarke, ed., *Architectural Stained Glass* (New York, 1979).

32 Andrew Moor, *Architectural Glass: A Guide for Design Professionals* (New York, 1989); id., *Architectural Glass Art: Form and Technique in Contemporary Glass* (New York, 1997).

33 Wassily Kandinsky, *Concerning the Spiritual in Art* (London, 1914 repr. New York/Dover, 1977); Maurice Tuchman, *The Spiritual in Art: Abstract Painting 1890–1985*, exh. cat., Los Angeles County Museum of Art (New York, 1986).

34 Sowers, *The Lost Art*, 63–65.

35 Ibid., 63.

36 Ibid., 67.

37 Robert Sowers, *Stained Glass: An Architectural Art* (New York, 1965), 7.

38 Sowers, *The Lost Art*, 67.

39 Sam Hunter, *Robert Rauschenberg* (New York, 1999), 86; Walter Hopps, *Robert Rauschenberg, A Retrospective* (New York, 1997).

40 Charles Jenks, *The Language of Post-Modern Architecture* (New York, 1984); id., *Architecture Today* (New York, 1982); Heinrich Klotz, *The History of Postmodern Architecture* (Cambridge, 1988); Diane Ghirardo, *Architecture after Modernism* (London, 1996); Hugh Pearman, *Contemporary World Architecture* (New York, 1998); James Steele, *Architecture Today* (New York, 1997).

2 THE OPALESCENT ERA:
THE NEW CENTURY BEGINS

A pane of dark blue and white, harsh and crude in reflected light, becomes suddenly glorious when seen in transmitted light, like a sunset all at once illuminating the sky in this land of rich effects.

Cecilia Waern, *The International Studio*, 1898[1]

Opalescent stained glass developed as a uniquely American phenomenon starting in the 1880s. At the turn of the century it dominated American creative expression. Its popularity corresponded to a taste for greater opulence in both domestic and public spaces. Luxuriant colors and textures, achieved by the use of inlays and veneers of marble and wood, wallpaper, stenciled painting, and leaded windows all combined for an unusually rich effect associated with what became known as the American Renaissance. The term evokes both the cultural coming of age of the United States and the importance of Italian and French Renaissance models in architecture and the decorative arts. Homes and public places alike showed a variety of elaborately cut, molded, and painted glass, often arranged in complex figural, floral or geometric designs. This brief essay will profile both the qualities of opalescent glazing – the nature of the material, the attraction of painters to it and the differences among the various studios – and the societal context that shaped the medium.

Artistic Climate of the American Renaissance

Art at the turn of the century was greatly influenced by the social issue of American newly acquired wealth. Opalescent windows were commissioned in the United States during the first gilded age by fabulously wealthy people who sought to validate their newly found status through a conspicuous display of culture. In this era, the collection of antique glass, the inspiration of new figural glass in an eclectic but predominantly Italian Renaissance mode, or the installation of richly patterned decorative work were treated alike. Stanford White (1853–1906), a partner in the firm of McKim, Mead, and White, architects of Boston's Public Library, collected and commissioned stained glass for himself and his clients.[2] The Payne Whitney House in New York City, the site of John La Farge's panel of *Autumn* (1902), was once also decorated with medieval glass that White had purchased on his European trips.[3] Charles Follen McKim (1847–1909), White's partner, installed medieval, German and Swiss Renaissance glass in the lavish library of J. Pierpont Morgan, constructed in New York City between 1902 and 1907 in a predominantly classical mode. Simply known to its visitors as the J. P. Morgan Library, it has been open to the public since 1924.

Like John La Farge (1835–1910), the designers for Louis Comfort Tiffany (1848–1933), as well as a host of imitators working at the turn of the century, sought to bring the stained glass into a closer alliance with painting. Tiffany, who founded what is perhaps the best known studio of the period, was born in 1848, the son of Charles Louis Tiffany, founder of the jewelry company, Tiffany & Company of New York.[4] The image of *Young Joseph* fabricated by the Tiffany Studios, Corona, New York, in this exhibition (figure 15) resembles a nineteenth-century salon painting, like Henri-Alexandre-Georges Regnault's *Salomé* (1870)

FIGURE 15

Louis Comfort Tiffany (1848–1933)

Fabricated by Tiffany Studios, Corona, NY

Young Joseph (detail), c. 1900

The Corning Museum of Glass, Corning, NY

FIGURE 16

Henri-Alexandre-Georges Regnault (1843–1871)

Salomé, **1870**

Metropolitan Museum of Art, New York City, NY

FIGURE 17
Louis Comfort Tiffany (1848–1933)

Fabricated by Tiffany Studios, Corona, NY

Young Joseph (detail), c. 1900

The Corning Museum of Glass, Corning, NY

(figure 16), a style that would have been popular among Tiffany's clients.[5] The youth's three-dimensional pose, the engagement of his gaze with the viewer, even the tactile quality of the yellow drapery-glass tunic (figure 17) set against the blue, green and purple "cloak of many colors"[6] compels our attention.

Glass in a New Form

Stained glass, whether inserted into a window, leaded into a lampshade or used to make a skylight or windows for a church or court, had become ubiquitous by the turn of the nineteenth century. For the very first time, large-scale, American architectural installations were aesthetically and materially linked to a history of glass making. America had a very long-standing tradition of quality production of the glass vessel, from the early days of the Sandwich Glass Company, Sandwich, Massachusetts, through the beveled and etched glass of the nineteenth century.[7] It is significant that Tiffany Glass and Decorating Company, the most prolific firm of this era, was equally at home with the production of the glass object, such as leaded lampshades and molded and blown vases as it was with the architectural

installation of a window.[8] The components of the glass were the same: richly variegated colors, sinuous forms, and the unmistakable milky colors and pearly sheen of the surface. In the case of the windows, their actual three-dimensional quality likened them even more to the glass vessels and light fixtures displayed within the home. A section of border from the Tiffany window (figure 18) suggests a rich incrustation of segments of glass. The density of color brings to mind the solid weight of sculpture. The use of textured glass, for jewels and drapery, evoked techniques of bas-relief linking the opalescent window with the carved reliefs in wood and stone of the buildings they adorned. The windows' colors and "glassiness" linked them with the glass objects set within those buildings such as the hanging lamps, vases, or paperweights.

The American development of variegated colors and surfaces within the material itself precipitated a discussion of the traditional role of paint on glass. Writers on stained glass began to question the usefulness of paint within this new style. Supporters of opalescent glass argued against it, as evident in Roger Riordan's 1881 analysis of a "Window in Pure Mosaic" by John La Farge:

In this sort of work the style should always be pure mosaic. There need be no lack of variety. Besides the endless combinations of geometrical forms, derivable from mediaeval designs, the Arabesque and Japanesque systems of abstract ornamentation are in practice drawn upon by all our designers. Mr. La Farge has led off with Renaissance designs in pure mosaic … The simple shapes of the lower animals and plants are easily imitated in this manner. Their forms may be indicated by the leading alone, or may be rendered with an almost illusive naturalness by the choice of wrinkled, bulging, and concave pieces of glass, as is done by Mr. Tiffany … Even in the case of the largest and most important work, the benefits conferred by enamel are, for the most part, obtainable also in mosaic. The partial opacity which it gives, at some artistic cost, can be got in the glass itself without any loss of surface quality. The legitimate use of enamel is thus reduced to the gaining of additional form by vigorous drawing in dark hatchings over the colored and self-shaded pot metal.[9]

Riordan's critique emphasized the role of pure glass and leadlines in the opalescent era against the traditional use of clear colored glass on which the artist applied painted designs. The issue of the nature of "true principles" of glass design – structural material versus paint – is at the core of artistic choices in stained glass, and still hotly debated today.

Glass as material continued to attract admirers in the opalescent era. In 1898, a popular writer on the arts of the period, Cecilia Waern (1853–after 1920), wrote on Louis Comfort Tiffany's Favrile glass for *The International Studio* (a monthly art and decorative magazine published between 1897 and 1931). She described in enthusiastic terms Tiffany's Corona glassworks (Jamaica, New York) with its stock of 200 to 300 tons of glass stored in cases and on numbered racks bringing order to the selection of 5,000 colors. The machine-rolled glass sheets appeared remarkable for their varieties of color.

A pane of dark blue and white, harsh and crude in reflected light, becomes suddenly glorious when seen in transmitted light, like a sunset all at once illuminating the sky in this land of rich effects… Other pieces suggest priceless onyx or lovely marbles, when seen in reflected light, shot through with throbbing color when held up to the window.[10]

FIGURE 18
Tiffany Glass & Decorating Company

Border Section from *Christ Blessing*, 1898

From Collegiate Church, New York, NY

On loan from Rohlf's Stained & Leaded Glass Mount Vernon, NY

Waern also described the hand-made glass that retained varying thickness, bubbles, and imperfections from the process of the throwing:

As many as seven different colours out of different ladles or spoons have been thrown together in this way … The throwing of certain masses and colour can be regulated, of course, and a definite design is often employed with a view to providing the glazier with 'useful' glass for obtaining certain effects of drapery, modeling or backgrounds … The famous Tiffany glass is made by manipulating the sheet while still hot, as one would do with pastry (with iron hooks, the hands cased in asbestos gloves) and pushing it together until it falls into folds.[11]

Tiffany's glass has been much discussed but rarely in the context of the wide popularity of opalescent glass and the many sources of opalescent glass production of the time. Recent publication of a portion of the archival information concerning Arthur J. Nash (1849–1834) and Leslie H. Nash (1884–1958), both of whom directed production of opalescent glass at the Corona glassworks for Tiffany, needs to be evaluated to profile the nature of collaboration in this field.[12] Before engaging Nash, Tiffany had experimented with glass in 1875 at Thill's Glasshouse, Brooklyn. Between 1880 and 1893 he used glass made expressly for him by the Heidt Glasshouse, also in Brooklyn. In 1892 he hired Arthur J. Nash, who had learned glassmaking in the Dennis Glass Work, near Stourbridge, England and built his own glass furnaces in Corona. In 1894 Tiffany registered the Favrile trademark. At this time, however, opalescent glass was already being produced elsewhere. The most significant producer of it was Kokomo Opalescent Glass, Kokomo, Indiana.

Kokomo Opalescent Glass was incorporated in 1888 and was managed by three partners – R. E. Hoss, President, J. W. Learner, Secretary, and W. E. Blacklidge. The company's economic advantage rested on what was once a huge pocket of natural gas. Discovered in the 1850s, the natural deposit extended from Ohio to Howard County, Indiana, and included most of the town of Kokomo. This resource provided ideal fuel for glass furnaces. The flourishing American market for glassware encouraged the founding of over ninety glass factories producing mostly glass vessels such as glasses, pitchers, vases and bowls. Kokomo Opalescent Glass, then known simply as "The Opalescent Glass Works," specialized in one-of-a-kind sheets of art glass. They sold not only to the burgeoning studio clientele, but to Tiffany as well. In 1893, even while the Corona factory was open, Tiffany purchased from Kokomo Opalescent Glass; one invoice lists almost 10,000 pounds of glass to "The Tiffany Glass Decorating Co."[13] When the gas source dried up a few years later, other smaller companies in the town closed, but Kokomo Opalescent survived. Today the company has the ability to manufacture over 22,000 different color/density/texture combinations, an indication of the variety that was available at the height of the opalescent era.

New Artists for an Old Medium

The opalescent era encouraged academically trained artists to design for glass. The out-of-house designer, as well as the studio with designers working exclusively in a team of glass cutters, painters, and fabricators, were also gaining prominence at this time. John La Farge, Louis Comfort Tiffany, and Maitland Armstrong (1836–1918), a painter and later a designer of stained glass, never actually touched the window. They may have provided designs and supervised execution, but they were not the artists who selected, cut and painted the glass, or assembled the window into its frame.

John La Farge is arguably one of the great innovators in the art of stained glass. He was born in New York on March 31, 1835, the son of John Frederick La Farge and Louisa Binsse de Saint

Victor, French émigrés. La Farge's early education was bilingual and emphasized literature and art. His Roman Catholic background encouraged a Catholic-affiliated schooling and he matriculated at Mount Saint Mary's College, Maryland, receiving a Masters' degree in 1855. Following this he studied law in New York while continuing to mingle in artistic circles. From 1856 to the fall of 1857 La Farge traveled in Europe, predominantly France and Belgium, familiarizing himself with the European tradition that would be so characteristic of his work.

La Farge's first successful window using the new material of opalescent glass was a domestic composition, *Morning Glories*, executed in 1878 for the William Watts Sherman house in Newport, Rhode Island, a summer haven for some of America's social elite.[14] La Farge combined selected stained glass in a variety of tones and a new material, an opalescent type of commercial glass previously used mainly as a porcelain substitute in toiletries such as brushes and mirrors. He filed for a patent for these techniques in November 1879.[15] La Farge's application makes it clear that he did not claim to invent the milky glass of variegated color we now call opalescent. Rather, he claimed a patent for its use in plated stained glass windows where areas of the window are comprised of several layers of glass stacked one on top of the other and leaded together. Plating adds depth to the play of color and light in the composition.

La Farge was seen as a designer of promise and in 1880 Herter Brothers, a decorating firm in New York, hired him to provide windows for the homes of American millionaires.[16] One of La Farge's first successful figural commissions in glass, the allegorical *The Fruits of Commerce* and *Hospitality/Prosperity*, was installed in the William H. Vanderbilt House in New York in 1881.[17]

Like La Farge, David Maitland Armstrong (1836–1918) was a painter in the first half of his life, producing carefully crafted landscapes of the Hudson River region and of Italy.[18] He was an intellectual, holding a law degree and an appointment as United States Consul to the Papal States, or Consul General to Rome. In 1872 he returned to the United States to pursue painting but soon developed a stronger interest in the applied arts. He was associated with Tiffany Studios from at least 1881 to 1887, after which he designed independently. Shortly before 1893 he formed his own firm, Armstrong and Company. His daughter, Helen Maitland Armstrong (1869–1948), began designing windows as early as 1894 and later became his partner in the firm.[19]

Armstrong, unlike La Farge, however, typically associated with other designers, first with the Associated Artists organized by Tiffany, discussed below, and then with his daughter, Helen. Armstrong's profile allows us to see how the expanded clientele for stained glass translated into a vastly expanded number of studios and artists designing for glass. In New York City, one of Armstrong's most impressive commissions is the Italian Renaissance style decorative schema for the dome and windows of the Appellate Court Building (1899).[20]

J & R Lamb Studios was founded in 1857 by English-born Joseph Lamb (1833–1898) and his brother Richard (1866–1888).[21] Located in New York City for eighty years, J & R Lamb Studios is considered the first American firm to specialize in all facets of ecclesiastical design.[22] At mid-century, the dominant style was the Gothic, particularly for the many Episcopalians. Since the 1830s, the Church of England had embraced a return to a more liturgically enriched worship, linked to the Middle Ages, and Episcopal churches in the United States followed suit. In the Northeast, the English-born architect and Gothicist Richard Upjohn (1802– 1878), a devoted Episcopalian, dominated ecclesiastic design.

J & R Lamb's early work concentrated on wood, stone, and textiles in the medieval revival mode. In 1876 an older son, Charles Rollinson Lamb

FIGURE 19
**Frederick Stymetz Lamb
(1863–1928)**
Religion Enthroned, **1899**
J & R Lamb Studios
Brooklyn Museum of Art,
Brooklyn, NY

(1860–1942), began designing and the firm expanded to include more variety in its styles, secular commissions, and work in stained glass, mosaics, and stone monuments. In 1885, Frederick Stymetz Lamb (1863–1928), Charles's younger brother, completed artistic studies at the Académie Julien in Paris and after returning to New York, he continued to paint in association with progressive artists such as George Inness (1825–1894), known for his landscape paintings. He also became aware of the opalescent experimentation of La Farge, whose fabricating studios were in proximity to the Lamb Studios. Influenced by La Farge's work, Frederick Lamb took his family's firm in the new direction. Frederick Lamb's career demonstrates the complexity of the schools at this time since he associated with people who could be categorized as part of two movements: Arts and Crafts and American Renaissance. Lamb executed work with the British designer Walter Crane (1845–1915) and the American furniture maker Gustav Stickley (1858–1942), authoring a number of articles for Stickley's magazine, *The Craftsman*. Frederick Lamb was also highly active in numerous organizations dedicated to the arts and their place in civic design. Opalescent glass was, indeed, the hallmark product of artists' studios at this time, seen in thousands of installations throughout the United States.

One of J & R Lamb's major commissions included over sixty windows installed between 1899 and 1903 for the Memorial Chapel of Stanford University, Stanford, California. Jane Stanford, the project's patron, planned the designs modeled on time-honored paintings of the life of Christ. Prints by Bernhard Plockhorst (1825–1907), Heinrich Hofmann (1824–1911), William Holman Hunt (1827–1910), and Gustave Doré (1832–1883), among others, were executed by the studio as complex, opalescent windows. Doré's *Dream of Pilate's Wife*, for example, was greatly enhanced by the opalescent depth given to the figures. Frederick Lamb's own design is seen in *Religion Enthroned* of 1899, a large

rectangular composition, now in the Brooklyn Museum. In the allegorical composition, Religion is seated on a Gothic throne flanked by standing winged female figures representing the Church Militant, clad in armor, and the Church Triumphant, dressed in long flowing robes.

The best-documented artist in the field, undoubtedly, is Louis Comfort Tiffany. His first association was with three other designers in 1879, Samuel Colman (1832–1920), Lockwood de Forest III (1869–1949), and Candace Wheeler (1827–1923) in the firm of Associated Artists.[23] In 1881–1882 the firm designed the interior of Mark Twain's sumptuous residence in Hartford, Connecticut and the Fifth Avenue mansions of Ogden Goelet and Cornelius Vanderbilt II in New York. Eclectic combinations of Japanese, Chinese, Moorish, and East Indian elements with those of the Italian Renaissance became an early signature of the firm.[24] Throughout his career Tiffany remained highly sensitive to the total environment; in his interiors windows, furniture and other decorative accessories are all considered.

In the second decade of the twentieth century the taste for opalescent glass began to wane, as simpler forms of Arts and Crafts and Art Deco began their ascendancy. The Second Gothic Revival, which began in the United States about 1910, championed medieval inspiration as the only appropriate style of windows. It challenged the appropriateness of the "picture window," a window done in the style of a painterly composition, for a religious edifice, and Tiffany Studios began a gradual decline. In 1932 it filed for bankruptcy and the following year Tiffany died at the age of eighty-four.

At the height of the Tiffany Studios' popularity, Tiffany oversaw a huge enterprise and willingly worked with other artists and designers, such as Edward Emerson Simmons (1852–1931) and Francis Davis Millet (1846–1912) for windows in Harvard University's Memorial Hall.[25] He also frankly acknowledged his adaptation of well-known paintings as the basis for stained glass designs, for example his *Seven Gifts of the Holy Spirit* after Sandro Botticelli's (1445–1510) *Virgin and Child Attended By Seven Angels* [26] and *Christ Leaving the Praetorium* by Gustave Doré.[27] In 1884 Tiffany entered into an agreement with Siegfried Bing, a Parisian art dealer, to fabricate windows after designs by French artists, including Pierre Bonnard, Maurice Denis, Henri de Toulouse-Lautrec, and Félix Vallotton, which Bing exhibited at his gallery, the "Salon de l'Art Nouveau" in 1885.[28] Many of the designers working for Tiffany, including Edward Peck Sperry (1850–1925), Rosina Emmett Sherwood (1854–1948), J. A. Holzer (1858– 1938), and Agnes Northrop (1857–1953), later worked independently.[29] The studio's most characteristic figural work, however, was indebted to Frederick Wilson (1858–1932), an Englishman who came to New York in the 1890s and stayed for over thirty years.[30]

Until the second decade of the twentieth century glass was so ubiquitous as an architectural element that it was impossible for an architect to design a building without considering the leaded window. Sometimes beveled and made of simple etched or frosted glass, or even unworked segments of machine-rolled glass, the idea of a stained glass window in the decorative scheme of an architectural structure was a reality. It is not surprising, then, to still see train stations, banks, court houses, libraries, and public auditoriums constructed to include stained glass windows. Virtually any city in America at the turn of the century could furnish examples of architectural installations of stained glass in commercial and domestic buildings: among them, the City Hall, Sheraton Palace Hotel, and Olympic Club, all in San Francisco; St. Louis's Union Station; or Pittsburgh's Lake Erie Railroad Terminal.

The very lavishness of these settings has endangered their survival. The upkeep of the complex carved, gilt, and colored surfaces demands extraordinary investment. Over time, these American Renaissance palaces fell out of favor as the lean lines of Art Deco and the even sparser embellishment of the Modern period captured public taste. Buildings fell into disuse, or, more disastrously, were renovated to accord with the growing aversion to opulence. These establishments began to look outdated, seedy, and less commercially attractive. The expense of repairing leaded windows and peeling paint over vast spaces of a railroad terminal could seem non-productive and even wasteful on a corporate balance sheet. Only with the rise of the Post Modern era have these great structures reclaimed their importance to owners and developers alike. The intermingling of styles from a variety of periods and the sensual delight in color and texture, indeed, even the confusion of materials and spaces created by the overload of surfaces resonate with the same challenges as those delighting the Post Modern designer. The reclaimed turn-of-the-century building now exists side by side with the recently built edifice of faux marble, truncated arcades, and floating pediments.

ENDNOTES

1 Cecilia Waern, *The International Studio*, 5 (New York, 1898), 17.

2 Two sales of White's collection were held in New York: *The Artistic Property Belonging to the Estate of the Late Stanford White to Be Sold at Unrestricted Public Sale on the Premises No. 121 East Twenty-first Street*, sale cat., American Art Association, 4–6 April (New York, 1907); *Illustrated Catalogue of Valuable Artistic Property, Collected by the Late Stanford White*, sale cat., American Art Association, 25–27 November (New York, 1907). See overview of the highlights of the collection in: *Stained Glass before 1700 in American Collections: Midwestern and Western States. Corpus Vitrearum Checklist* III, ed. and intro. Madeline H. Caviness/Jane Hayward, Studies in the History of Art, 28 (Washington, 1989), 14.

3 Now the French Cultural Embassy. H. Barbara Weinberg, *The Decorative Works of John La Farge* (New York, 1977), 417–19. For additional insights into White's eclectic manner see the analysis of Harbor Hill, Roslyn, Long Island, New York by Lawrence Wodehouse, "Stanford White and the Mackays: A Case Study in Architect – Client Relationships," *Winterthur Portfolio,* 11 (1976): 213–33.

4 Louis became a design director of Tiffany & Company on the death of his father. A number of designs appear in both glass windows by Tiffany Studios and enamels by Tiffany & Company, such as the *Four Seasons*. See essays by Alastair Duncan/Martin Eidelberg/Neil Harris, *Masterworks of Louis Comfort Tiffany*, exh. cat., National Museum of American Art, Washington D.C. (New York, 1989), 133, fig. 54; Robert Koch, *Louis C. Tiffany. Rebel in Glass* (New York, 1964, 2nd ed. 1966).

5 Given to the Metropolitan Museum of Art in 1916. Gift of George F. Baker, 16.95.

6 Genesis 37.3 (King James Version).

7 Jane Shadel Spilman and Susanne K. Franz, *Masterpieces of American Glass*, exh. cat., The Corning Museum of Glass (New York, 1990).

8 Hugh McKean, *The "Lost Treasures" of Louis Comfort Tiffany* (Garden City, 1980); Alice Cooney Frelinghuysen, "Louis Comfort Tiffany at the Metropolitan Museum," *Bulletin of the Metropolitan Museum of Art,* 56 (1998).

9 Roger Riordan, "American Stained Glass," pts. 1–3, *American Art Review* 2/2 (1881): 61–62, ill.

10 Cecila Waern, "The Industrial Arts of America: II, The Tiffany or Favrile Glass," *The International Studio* 5 (1898): 16–21, quote 17.

11 Ibid., 17–18.

12 Martin Eidelberg/Nancy A. McClelland, ed., *Behind the Scenes of Tiffany Glassmaking: The Nash Notebooks* (New York, 2000).

13 Archives of Kokomo Opalescent Glass, Kokomo, Indiana.

14 Now in the collection of the Museum of Fine Arts, Boston, 1974.498 a-f, gift of James F. and Jean Baer O'Gorman; Henry Adams, *John La Farge*, exh. cat., The Carnegie Museum of Art and the National Museum of American Art, Smithsonian Institution (New York, 1987), 197–98, fig. 145.

15 Weinberg, *Decorative Works*, 357–72 argues convincingly for the primacy of La Farge's technical inventions. See also id., "John La Farge's and the Invention of American Opalescent Windows," *Stained Glass* 67/3 (1972): 4–11.

16 Katherine S. Howe et al., *Herter Brothers: Furniture and Interiors for a Gilded Age*, exh. cat., Museum of Fine Arts, Houston/Metropolitan Museum of Art, New York (New York, 1994).

17 Now in the Biltmore House, Asheville, North Carolina. See Adams, ed., *John La Farge*, 199–200, figs. 146–47 and Weinberg, *Decorative Work*, 268–72, figs. 206–10.

18 See autobiographic statement, D. Maitland Armstrong, *Day Before Yesterday: Reminiscences of a Varied Life* (New York, 1920). The work was edited by his daughter Margaret after Armstrong's death in 1918.

19 Robert O. Jones, "Maitland Armstrong & Company: Uncatalogued Windows in the South Reveal Studio's Superb Artistry," *Stained Glass* 81 (Winter 1986), 288–93.

20 Robert O. Jones, "New York Appellate Court Building: Armstrong Windows of the 'American School'," *Stained Glass* (Summer 1991), 124–29.

21 David Adams, "Frederick S. Lamb's Opalescent Vision of 'A Broader Art': The Reunion of Art and Craft in Public Murals," in: Bert Denker, ed., *The Substance of Style: Perspectives on the American Arts and Crafts Movement* (Winterthur, 1996), 317–40; John R. Burger, "How America's Oldest Studio Remains Creative Today," *Stained Glass* (Fall 1977), 168–70.

22 See Phoebe Stanton, *The Gothic Revival and American Church Architecture: An Episode of Taste, 1840–1856* (Baltimore/London, 1968); Everard M. Upjohn, *Richard Upjohn, Architect and Churchman* (New York, 1968).

23 See Wilson H. Faude, "Associated Artists and the American Renaissance in the Decorative Arts," *Winterthur Portfolio* 10 (1975), 101–30.

24 Neil Harris, "In Search of Influence," in: Duncan, Eidelberg/ Harris, *Masterworks of Louis Comfort Tiffany*, 14–48; Marilyn Johnson, "The Artful Interior," in: Doreen Bolger Burke, et al., *In Pursuit of Beauty*, exh. cat., Metropolitan Museum of Art (New York, 1986), 111–41.

25 Millet's *Student and Soldier*, 1889 and *General Joseph Warren and Reverend John Eliot*, 1889: *Harvard College Class of 1861; Fifth Report* (1892), frontispiece; Simmons's *Aristides and Themistocles*, 1892: *Harvard College Class of 1874, Seventh Report* (1899) 159–61, illustrated, Harvard University Archives; *List of Tiffany Glass*, Tiffany Studios, 1910, John H. Sweeney, ed. (Watertown, 1972), 66.

26 The Morse Gallery of Art, Winter Park, Florida, 1885; see McKean, *The Lost Treasures* (Garden City, 1980), fig. 47. Botticelli's painting is also known as the *Madonna dei Candelabri*, ca. 1485, now in Berlin, Staatliche Museen.

27 St. Paul's Episcopal Church, Milwaukee, 1888; see Alastair Duncan, *Tiffany Windows* (New York, 1980), fig. 7.

28 Duncan, *Tiffany Windows*, 105–112. Gabriel P. Weisberg, Art *Nouveau Bing: Paris Style 1900* (New York, 1986), esp. 44–79, and id., "S. Bing in America," in: Gabriel P. Weisberg/ Laurina S. Dixon, ed., *The Documented Image. Visions in Art History* (Syracuse, 1987), 51–68.

29 Duncan, *Tiffany Windows*, 65–74.

30 Virginia C. Raguin, *Glory in Glass*, 205–7.

3

Nothing is more annoying to me than
any tendency toward realism of form
in window glass.

Frank Lloyd Wright, *In the Cause of Architecture*, 1928.[1]

The early years of the twentieth century witnessed different stylistic movements occurring simultaneously in the design of stained glass. Several, like the style of Frank Lloyd Wright and Art Deco, were primarily guided by architectural priorities. The Art Nouveau and Arts and Crafts movements, however, were linked to a broader trend in decorative arts that encompassed work in furniture, tableware, wall paper, illustration, jewelry, and dress that afforded the artists considerable commissions and allowed the patron a wide range of acquisitions in a similar form and philosophy. All of these movements shared an intense interest in the materials themselves and, regarding stained glass, the exploitation of light and transparency as well as color. The following chapter traces the ways in which each responded to these artistic issues.

Arts and Crafts and Art Deco

Arts and Crafts and Art Deco influenced architecture and the decorative arts but were indifferently represented in the "fine arts" of painting in Europe and the United States. The United Kingdom (Scotland, Ireland, and England) experienced a turn-of-the century revival of Arts and Crafts, and this work is represented in American buildings. For example, the glass studio of Daniel Cottier (1838–91), Glasgow, Scotland, installed windows in Trinity Church, Boston; Irish artists completely filled the windows of the Jesuit Brophy College Chapel, in Phoenix, Arizona; and Christopher and Veronica

Whall, of London, produced glass for the former chapel of Rosemary Hall, Greenwich, Connecticut.

At the same time artists in the United States were independently developing a new sense of the post-opalescent design possibilities. Chief among them were Otto Heinigke (1850–1915) of New York and Harry Eldredge Goodhue (1873–1918), the brother of architect Bertram G. Goodhue (1869–1924), a partner in the architectural firm of Cram, Goodhue and Ferguson, (Ralph Adams Cram (1863–1942), Frank W. Ferguson (1861–1926)), Boston. Heinigke and H. E. Goodhue's art stressed the two-dimensional nature of the window and strong surface graphic, distinguishing themselves from the Victorian realism and sentimentality so characteristic of the opalescent windows produced at the time.

For example, Heinigke's designs, as evident in the angels and apostles in Philadelphia's First Baptist Church (1900), are elegantly attenuated through flat segments of intense color.[2] H.E. Goodhue's two windows dating to 1905, for the east aisle of All Saints, Brookline, Massachusetts, contrast male and female figures from Scripture: Joshua, the archangel Michael, and Gideon, and Mary Magdalene, Mary, the mother of Jesus, and Elizabeth (figures 20, 21).[3] The clarity of color and abstraction of the modeling enhance the sweeping drama of the gestures. Pioneering artistic statements in glass such as these made the American stained glass field receptive for progressive tendencies that

Joshua The Son Of Nun

St Michael Archangel

Gideon Son Of Joash

"A Good Man Leaveth

An Inheritance To His

Children's Children

FIGURE 20

Harry Eldridge Goodhue (1873–1918)

Joshua, Archangel Michael, and Gideon, 1905

Timothy Corey Memorial Window

All Saints Church, Brookline, MA

FIGURE 21

Harry Eldridge Goodhue (1873–1918)

Mary Magdalene, detail from *Biblical Heroines* window, 1905

Sarah Elizabeth Corey Memorial Window

All Saints Church, Brookline, MA

were to come from abroad. Impressive installations like Heinigke and H. E. Goodhue's, combined with their publications, deeply influenced later American work.[4]

In Ireland the revival of glass painting coincided with a revival of nationalism and a reverence for the decorative arts exemplified by the medieval Celtic tradition (eighth through tenth centuries). Christopher Whall (1849–1925), England's most eloquent spokesman of the Arts and Crafts movement and the author of a widely read text, *Stained Glass Work*, visited Ireland. He subsequently sent over his chief assistant Alfred Ernest Child (1875–1939) to take up an appointment in September 1901 as instructor in Stained Glass at the Dublin Metropolitan School of Art. With the support of the artist and philanthropist Sarah Purser (1848–1943), Child helped organize *An Túr Gloine* (Irish for "The Tower of Glass") which operated from 1903 to 1944. The Irish translation of the studio's name was itself chosen to emphasize Irish national pride rooted in its medieval Celtic past. Almost all significant Irish artists in stained glass, including Wilhelmina Geddes (1887–1955) and Michael Healy (1873–1941), were at some time associated with the workshop, which was inspired by William Morris's (1834–1896) philosophy of the value of craft to the modern world.[5] The artists of *An Túr Gloine* declared that:

each window should be in all its artistic parts the work of one individual artist, the glass chosen and painted by the same mind and hand that made the design and drew the cartoon, in fact a bit of stained glass should be a work of free art as much as any painting or picture.[6]

This rigorous statement was modified to permit collaboration, however, for a number of important commissions, secured in the United States were collaborative. For example, *An Túr Gloine* executed windows of the *Patron Saints of Music* in 1933 for St. Vincent Ferrer Church, New York City, after a design by Charles Connick.[7] Harry Clarke (1889–1931), one of the most important of the *An Túr Gloine* artists, also designed windows for the United States, including nine chancel windows installed in 1929 in the Basilica of St. Vincent de Paul in Bayonne, New Jersey.[8]

Publications such as Whall's insured that these principles of artistic creativity espoused by *An Túr Gloine* reached the United States. In *Stained Glass Work* he argued that for a window to be successful, the studio system must be altered to allow greater communication among all aspects of a window's fabrication: sketching of an initial window design; drawing the cartoon; choosing, cutting and painting the glass; and finally leading the glass into the window. Whall encouraged the studio owner to "keep his hand of mastery over the whole work personally at all stages."[9]

Whall was involved in many facets of production of windows in his studio. For example, he began to use Prior's Early English or Slab Glass, developed in 1889 by the firm of Britten & Gilson at the suggestion of the architect E. S. Prior. Unusually thick and uneven, "Early English" glass encouraged emphasis on the color and texture of the glass itself and discouraged overly fussy painting onto the glass's uneven surface. Whall exploited the nature of the new glass, eschewing painting methods so popular at the time, to produce windows striking for their color contrasts. His masterpiece is generally accepted to be the windows in the Lady Chapel and Chapter House of Gloucester Cathedral, England (figure 22) depicting the saints and story of salvation, showing his predilection for clear colors and large expanses of white glass juxtaposed with intense, streaky red and blue.[10]

Windows produced by Whall for two churches in the United States heralded the new style on American shores:[11] *Christ in Glory* (or the *Risen Christ*) flanked by Saints Peter and John the

FIGURE 22
**Christopher Whall
(1849–1925)**

Virgin Annunciate
(detail), 1901

Lady Chapel, Gloucester
Cathedral, England

Evangelist, installed in 1905, in All Saints Church, Ashmont, Massachusetts and windows depicting the *Church Fathers* in the clerestory of the Church of the Advent, Boston, installed in 1910. All Saints Church was designed by the architect Ralph Adams Cram and built between 1892 and 1895. It is recognized today as the first major example of the twentieth-century Gothic Revival architecture in the United States. The clean lead lines, the clarity of the "Early English" glass and the contrast between the saturated palate of the deep red and blue glass and bright white glass Whall employed in *Christ in Glory* exemplifies the sobriety, and the love of sensual materials that permeates Cram's building. Whall's work is notable for the treatment of paint on glass. He applied paint to enhance the inherent quality of glass as a medium through which light was transmitted. The result is windows where glass, not paint on glass, is emphasized.

The young Charles Connick, who viewed All Saints and the Advent windows before they were placed high in the buildings, was deeply impressed by Whall's clarity of materials and the dignity of his figures.[12] Connick emphasized both characteristics in his own window of Saints Stephen, Paul, Peter and James, dedicated to the memory of George H. Champlin, in All Saints Church, Brookline, Massachusetts, 1910 (figures 23, 24).[13] The intense graphic power of the design equalizes the surface tension among color and white glass. An equally eloquent tribute to Whall is Connick's *The Holy Grail* window of 1919 for Cram and Ferguson's Proctor Hall, Princeton University.[14]

Advocates of the Arts and Crafts movement collected individual works as well as commissioned installations. In 1925, George G. Booth (1864–1949), the prominent patron of the Detroit Institute of Arts and the founder of the Cranbrook Academy in Bloomfield Hills, Michigan, acquired stained glass by Connick and by Michael Healy. Connick supplied Booth with several examples of his own work,

FIGURE 23

**Charles J. Connick
(1875–1945)**

*Saints Stephen, Paul,
Peter, and James*, 1910

George Hobron
Champlin Memorial
Window

All Saints Church,
Brookline, MA

FIGURE 24

**Charles J. Connick
(1875–1945)**

St. Stephen (detail)

George Hobron
Champlin Memorial
Window

All Saints Church,
Brookline, MA

FIGURE 25

Thomas Augustin O'Shaughnessy (1870–1956)

For the Glory of God, after 1912

Old St. Patrick's Church, Chicago, IL

replicas of an Arts and Crafts style window made for the bishop's private chapel in the Washington Cathedral and a more Gothic Revival style window for Grove Cemetery in Salem, Massachusetts.[15]

An original American interpretation of Arts and Crafts/Art Nouveau style is the work of Thomas Augustin O'Shaughnessy (1870–1956),[16] represented in this exhibition by two inscription panels in opalescent glass. The inscription panels read *For the Glory of God* (figure 25) and *For the Love of Mankind*.[16] Beginning in 1912 O'Shaughnessy installed over eighty new windows for St. Patrick's Church (now called Old St. Patrick's). Built between 1852 and 1856, it stands as the oldest religious building in Chicago.[17] The nave windows depict Irish saints in a three-dimensional painterly style vaguely similar to La Farge's oplascent figural windows. For example, O'Shaughnessy renders drapery like La Farge sculpting fabric folds in glass. Both men exploited the shape of the leaded glass pieces and subtle color variation inherent in opalescent glass to suggest the drape and fall of fabric. Ornamental panels frame the nave windows at the top and bottom. O'Shaughnessey's inspirations for

the ornament were the Celtic designs exhibited at the 1893 *World's Columbian Exposition* in Chicago, in "Lady Aberdeen's Irish Village" and his study in Dublin of manuscripts such as the ninth century *Book of Kells*. In 1921 O'Shaughnessy installed three balcony windows in Old St. Patrick's on the theme of the Theological virtues of Faith, Hope and Charity (figure 26) relying even more on Art Nouveau inspiration.

Art Deco and the Second Gothic Revival

The term "Art Deco" derives from the 1925 *Paris Exposition Internationale des Arts Décoratifs Industriels et Modernes*, which focused on contemporary design in both fine arts and everyday life. Though Art Deco objects often exhibit eclectic origins, they generally share characteristics of geometry and simplicity often combined with clear shapes and vibrant colors. Stained glass, with its linear patterns and brilliant hues, was particularly suited to the Art Deco aesthetic.

Hallmarks for the Art Deco style are the streamlined qualities of industrial production, often evoking the modern world of speed and aerodynam-

FIGURE 26
**Thomas Augustin
O'Shaughnessy
(1870–1956)**

Balcony window, 1921

Old St. Patrick's Church,
Chicago, IL

FIGURE 27

Artist unknown

***Stylized Plant Border*, 1930s**

Collection Conrad Schmitt Studios

New Berlin, WI

ics. Thus New York's great Art Deco skyscrapers speak to the power of industrial design and pride in American technology. The Chrysler Building, for instance, was designed in 1930 by William van Alen (1883–1954) to reflect the lines of the Chrysler automobile, down to its facing of Nircosta metal, which resembles platinum. The Empire State Building's tiered structure repeats geometric patterns so typical of Art Deco style that held sway throughout the 1920s and 1930s.

Art Deco inspiration also coincided with the influence of the second Gothic Revival, producing some impressive hybrids discussed in the following chapter. Authors from Otto Heinigke to Charles Connick described the importance of medieval windows as an inspiration for modern design. The dominance of blue and red in French thirteenth-century stained glass windows, such as those of Chartres cathedral, were often seen as a natural, and even mandated design choice for windows placed in religious buildings.

Several windows in this exhibition produced in the 1930s to 1940s exemplify stylistic principles of the time. Though their origins are uncertain, the windows' style suggests that they were made for ecclesiastic settings. In looking at the *Stylized Plant Border* (figure 27), the density of color and the strong prominence of blue counterbalanced by red with white and gold touches suggest that it was destined for a church. The graphic of the design is totally integrated into the structure of the leadline. The panel of *Wheat and Grapes* (figure 28), shows a bold adaptation of geometry to natural forms. Designed as ten evenly spaced circles, the grapes nestle within an isosceles triangle. The wheat sheaf displays alternating gold and white stripes in a narrowing triangle. Manipulated with delicate cross-hatching, the backgrounds are also enhanced by the variegated thickness and opacity of the glass. The very simplicity of the design draws attention to the quality of the materials, producing a highly successful exploitation

of glass as a medium of content and of aesthetic import. Most importantly, the spiritual meaning of the wine and bread in Christian communion is reiterated by the presence of transfigured light.

The *Bible Window* (figure 29) is a demonstration panel for ten windows designed around 1943 for the Cathedral of the Holy Spirit, Bismarck, North Dakota. Ground was broken in 1941 and the cathedral was under construction through 1945 due to the restrictions of the war years. An Art Deco style was the choice of architect William Kurke, Fargo, North Dakota, who commissioned the windows from the firm of Weston and Leighton of Minneapolis, Minnesota.[19] The symbol of the open book can be seen in the upper right corner; the cathedral's windows represent other symbols of the history of salvation. The predominant themes of the Bible window are mountain and rainbow shapes, evoking the Convenant of God with his people after the flood: "I will set my bow in the clouds, and it shall be the sign of a covenant between me, and between the earth." (Genesis, 9.13). The intersection of the simplest forms of the circle and the right angle constitute the elemental principles of the window, very much like a Mondrian painting with its primary colors and rectangular shapes.

Thistle Border, (figure 30) dating from the 1930's, displays a sense of both Art Nouveau curves and Art Deco abstraction. The subtle balance of color integrates both background and motif into an interlocking harmony. Green and red are complementary colors – polar opposites on the color wheel, a juxtaposition of the two increases the viewer's sensitivity to each. But rather than emphasize such a sharp dichotomy, the artist has selected muted tones of these colors, allowing for both the colors' vivacity and reciprocity. The elemental geometric abstraction and interest in organic forms that the above-cited windows illustrate were also issues that fascinated architects.

FIGURE 28

Artist unknown

Wheat and Grapes,
1930s

Collection Conrad
Schmitt Studios

New Berlin, WI

FIGURE 29

Weston and Leighton

Bible Window, **c. 1943**

Cathedral of the Holy
Spirit, Bismarck, ND

Collection Gaytee
Stained Glass

Minneapolis, MN

FIGURE 30

Artist unknown

Thistle Border, **1930s**

Collection Gaytee
Stained Glass

Minneapolis, MN

Frank Lloyd Wright's (1859–1967) position as an artist of stained glass windows does not fall easily into the previously discussed categories, primarily because his windows are almost exclusively secular and designed for his own buildings (figure 31). His work, however, is linked to his contemporaries' developments in many ways. During the early years of the twentieth century, there may have been a "revolt against Art Nouveau" in some quarters, as characterized by architectural historian Vincent Scully (1920–), but the lessons of total design were not forgotten.[20] The Art Nouveau interior had deeply impressed European and American sensibilities, especially its unity in the arts and design concepts that could link furniture, architecture, and windows in a coordinated whole.[21]

Wright's work in glass is grounded in his sensibility as an architect. He designed windows as an integral part of a finely conceived spatial aesthetic, a direction he inherited from his six years working directly under Louis Sullivan (1856–1924) at the Chicago architectural firm of Adler and Sullivan. Sullivan's work involved extensive design of stained glass in many buildings, exemplified by Chicago's Auditorium Hotel and Theater (now Roosevelt University), in 1889.[22] Sullivan's inspiration was curvilinear; Wright's, as seen in his famous Prairie style houses, was rectilinear, inspired by the low horizontal lines of the prairie on which they sat.[23] Their long rows of casement windows under low-pitched roofs further emphasized the horizontal theme.

Wright's inspiration led other Chicago architects to work in what has often been referred to as the "Prairie School" manner. An opalescent window in this exhibition uses Prairie-school principles in the wheat sheaf pattern – or Tree of Life – so common to Wright's work (figure 32). The brown tonalities come from the Arts and Crafts tradition. Unlike Wright's windows of predominantly clear glass, the opalescent pattern structures the surface while restricting view to the outside. Windows for religious spaces most often screen the interior from exterior distractions, permitting only filtered light to enter the space of worship. The wheat sheaf pattern was often seen as a religious theme. Even congregations that did not hold Communion as a central ritual reflected on the life-giving nature of bread in both the Old and the New Testament. Often abstract patterns were combined in churches with some kind of image, such as medallions showing an open Bible, a cross and crown, or even a realistically rendered portrait of Christ.

Ecclesiastic buildings were rare in Wright's work, although his own father had been a Unitarian minister. One notable exception was the Unity Temple, Oak Park, Illinois constructed between 1906 and 1909.[24] The twenty clerestory windows form a horizontal band around the upper portion of the building allowing the skylight segments to repeat the geometric plan of the building itself. Wright was concerned that the window be functional, allowing light and, when opened, air to circulate, as well as the object of attractive decorative materials. For him,

nothing is more annoying to me than any tendency toward realism of form in window glass, to get mixed up with the view outside. A window pattern should stay severely 'put.'

Wright qualified this statement by adding that,

The magnificent window-painting and plating of the windows of the religious edifice is quite another matter. There the window becomes primarily a gorgeous painting – painting with light itself.[25]

Wright's ability to develop an interaction between interior and exterior forms through a screen of glass is exemplified in his design of the stairwell window for the Susan Lawrence Dana House, in Springfield, Illinois.[26] Patterns of quickly shifting small rectangles cluster at the lancet heads and appear again as a

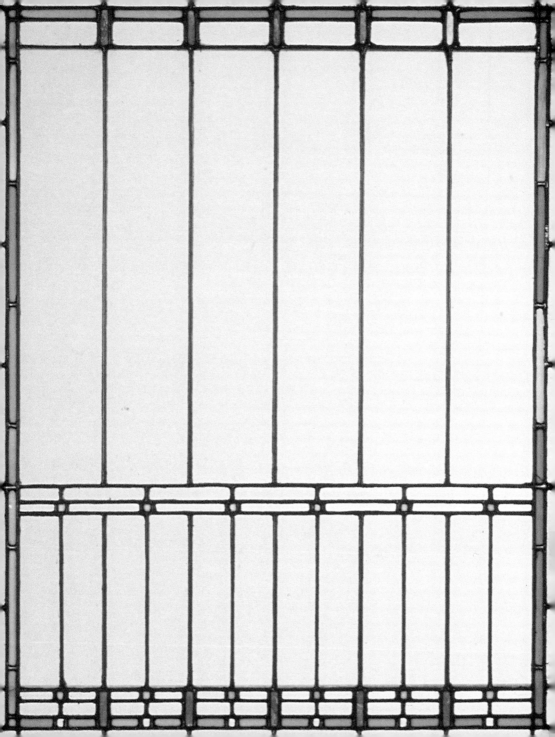

FIGURE 31

**Frank Lloyd Wright
(1859–1967)**

Bedroom Window

Francis W. Little House,
Peoria, NY

FIGURE 32

Artist unknown

**Opalescent "Prairie
Style" Border, 1910–20**

Collection Gaytee
Stained Glass

Minneapolis, MN

minor echo at the base. The tall narrow lancets, whose verticality is emphasized by the thrust of the leadlines, "stay put" as architectural elements, repeating the vertical shapes of the house and the rectangular patterns of the interior furnishings.

A comparison with European experience with Art Nouveau, particularly in Barcelona, places Wright's work in some perspective.[27] At the same time that Wright was designing his Prairie Houses, three architects, Josep Puig I Cadafalch (1867–1956), Antonio Gaudi (1862–1926), and Lluís Domènech i Montaner (1849–1923) were active in Barcelona and the surrounding cities of Catalonia, Spain. Rigorously Art Nouveau (in Catalonia, called *Modernist*), buildings designed by Domènech i Montaner emphasize organic forms and combine sculpture, architecture, and surface decoration into an indistinguishable unity. Planned in 1902 and under construction until 1930, his Hospital de Sant Pau (figure 33) is a vast complex of patterned pavilions.[28] The entrance building is dominated by a great vaulted ceiling, glazed cupolas, and open and blind clerestories, creating large open spaces set against narrow corridors. The windows incorporate both clear panes and leaded elements of translucent organic form whose patterns reflect those of the painted walls and the ceramic inlays. Similarly, Montaner's Palace of Catalan Music, built between 1905 and 1908, combines extensive use of stained glass, including a huge inverted cupola in the auditorium, and leaded wall dividers and screens throughout. Light both penetrates and is diffused by the glass and the polychrome ceramic mosaic of the exterior and interior.

The Arts and Crafts movement urged the integration of similar design principles and materials into all buildings, whether a country villa, suburban home, public auditorium, or religious edifice. As such, it paralleled the aesthetics of the Opalescent Era. Indeed, American Arts and Crafts glazing installations paralleled opalescent glass chronologically,

so it is truly problematic to define a strong division between the two. Art of the early decades of the twentieth century strove to become an integral part of life. The same forms in the home, law court, or the church were meant to blend private and public areas of social activity. The phrase "redesigning the world" to describe the goals of the English Arts and Crafts movement is equally appropriate for the American observations such as those of Frank Lloyd Wright and Arts and Crafts designers discussed above.[29] Significantly, the thrust of the movement in America gravitated strongly toward abstract patterns, most brilliantly observable in architectural ornament, furniture, pottery, textiles, and jewelry.[30] Wright emerged from this period as one of few great creators of leaded windows, and his strength is the abstract linearity of the design. The need of windows to carry a didactic meaning, however, especially for religious edifices, remained at issue and encouraged new developments. Springing from Arts and Crafts origins, the Second Gothic Revival soon appeared to claim almost exclusive superiority for religious edifices or decorative programs designed for them.

FIGURE 33

**Lluís Domènech i
Montaner (1849–1923)**

**Entrance Pavilion,
1902–1930**

Hospital de Sant Pau,
Barcelona, Spain

ENDNOTES

1 Frank Lloyd Wright, *In the Cause of Architecture*, (New York, 1975), 66.

2 See Virginia C. Raguin, *Glory in Glass*, 119–22, 183–85.

3 Richard Thomas Montross, "The Windows of All Saints Parish," 1982, typescript.

4 Otto Heinigke, "Architectural Sympathy in Leaded Glass," *Architectural Review* 4/7 (1896): 60–64; id., "Rambling Thoughts of a 'A Glass Man'," *Craftsman* 3 (1902): 170–82, reprinted in *Stained Glass* 30/4 (1935–36), 75–90. Harry Eldredge Goodhue, "Stained Glass in Private Houses," *Architectural Record* 18 (1905), 347–54; id., "Stained Glass," *Handicraft* 2 (July 1903), 76–92.

5 Charles A. Sewter, *The Stained Glass of William Morris and His Circle* (New Haven, 1974).

6 *An Túr Gloine: Anniversary Booklet* (Dublin, 1928), 9, as quoted by Nicola Gordon Bowe/David Caron/Michael Wynne, *Gazetteer of Irish Stained Glass: The Works of Harry Clarke and the Artists of An Túr Gloine, (The Tower of Glass) 1903–1963* (Dublin, 1998), 19.

7 Ibid., 87. The window is above the organ in the chancel and takes its place in the midst of a complete Connick program.

8 Nicola Gordon Bowe, *The Life and Works of Harry Clarke* (Dublin, 1989).

9 Christopher Whall, *Stained Glass Work: A Textbook for Students and Workers in Glass*, in: W. R. Lethaby, ed., *Arts and Crafts Series of Technical Handbooks* (New York, 1905), 268–69.

10 David Welander, *The Stained Glass of Gloucester Cathedral* (Gloucester, 1985), 114–30, illustrated; Christopher Whall, *Stained Glass Work*, pls. XI, XII, XVI; Charles J. Connick, "Modern Glass – A Review," *International Studio* 80, No 329 (1924), 41.

11 Peter Cormack, "Christopher Whall," *Stained Glass* 76 (1981–82), 320–21.

12 Connick examined other windows by Whall during his 1910 visit to Europe: Charles J. Connick "1910 Notebook", Charles J. Connick Collection, Archives of American Art, Smithsonian Institution. Noreen O'Gara, "Retrospective … Charles J. Connick," *Stained Glass* (Spring 1987), 44–49, 59–61, with chronology; id. "Charles J. Connick: The Early Years," Masters thesis, Tufts University, 1988; Orin E. Skinner, "Connick in Retrospect," *Stained Glass* 70 (Spring 1975), 16–19. For early work by Connick, see windows of Boston University's Chapel in: Daniel March, *The Charm of the Chapel* (Boston, 1950); windows in St. John's Episcopal Church, Beverly Farms, Massachusetts, in: Bronwyn Evans Loring, *St. John's Stained Glass* (privately printed, 1985); and windows of Calvary Episcopal Church, Pittsburgh, Pennsylvania in: Virginia L. Garland, "American History in Stained Glass at Calvary Episcopal Church, Pittsburgh, Pennsylvania," *Stained Glass* 71 (Fall 1976), 146–53. Windows from Connick's "Whall" period are in the nave of St. Paul's Episcopal Cathedral, Detroit, Michigan.

13 Noreen O'Gara, "Retrospective," 44–46; Richard Thomas Montross, "The Windows of All Saints Parish."

14 The window was immediately "textualized" in "The Holy Grail Window, Proctor Hall, Graduate College, Princeton University," *Stained Glass*, 13/2 (1919), 7–11. The article lists all the craftspersons in the studio as well as Connick. See also, Virginia C. Raguin, *Glory in Glass*, 114–15.

15 Connick's panels include *Fortitude of Job* CAAM 1925.1 (replica of windows installed 1921/22 in Harmony Grove Cemetery Chapel, Salem, Massachusetts). See Noreen O'Gara, Masters thesis, 48–49, fig. 6 (note 2), and *St. Genevieve of Paris and St. Ursula of Cologne* CAAM 1925.4 (replica of window installed about 1921/22 in the Bishop's Private chapel, Episcopal Cathedral, Washington, D. C.).

16 See T. J. Edelstein, ed., *Imagining an Irish Past: The Celtic Revival 1840–1940*, exh. cat., The David and Alfred Smart Museum of the University of Chicago (Chicago, 1992), 154–57.

17 Erne R. Frueh/Florence Frueh, *Chicago Stained Glass* (Chicago, 1983), 66–69.

18 When Conrad Schmitt Studios, New Berlin, Wisconsin conserved the windows in the 1990s, they were asked to hold the windows for future incorporation into new windows for the Chapel of Reservation. Because the windows were placed back to back in their original location and were very difficult to read as a result, the church preferred not to re-install them. Communication from Bernard Gruenke, Conrad Schmitt Studio.

19 Communication from Father Thomas Kramer, Cathedral of the Holy Spirit, Bismarck, North Dakota.

20 Vincent Scully, Jr., *Modern Architecture* (New York, 1974), 24.

21 See, James F. O'Gorman, *Three American Architects: Richardson, Sullivan, and Wright. 1865–1915* (Chicago, 1991), esp. 141–44.

22 Erne R. Frueh/Florence Frueh, *Chicago Stained Glass*, 48–52; Roosevelt University, *Windows to the Millenium*, October 2000 through April 2001, exhibition organized by Adrienne Hirsch; Guide by Kathleen Cummings.

23 David Larkin and Bruce Brooks Pfeiffer, ed., *Frank Lloyd Wright: The Masterworks* (New York, 1993), 34–103.

24 Joseph M. Siry, *Unity Temple: Frank Lloyd Wright and Architecture for Liberal Religion* (Cambridge/New York, 1996), esp. 166–69.

25 Frank Lloyd Wright, "In the Cause of Architecture. VI, The Meaning of Materials, Glass," *The Architectural Record* (1928); reprinted id., *In the Cause of Architecture*, ed. Frederick Gutheim (New York, 1975), 197–202, quote 201.

26 For these and other windows see Julie L. Sloan, *Light Screens: The Complete Leaded-Glass Windows of Frank Lloyd Wright* (New York, 2001). See also H. Allen Brooks, *Frank Lloyd Wright and the Prairie School*, exh. cat., Cooper-Hewitt Museum (New York, 1984).

27 Joan Vila-Grau/Francesc Rodon, "Vitralls modernists catalans," in: *El Vitrall Modernista*, exh. cat., Fundacio Joan Miro (Barcelona, 1984), 21–38; Lluís Domènech Girbau, *Lluís Domènech i Montaner* (Barcelona, 1994).

28 See Robert Hughes, *Barcelona* (New York, 1992), esp. 391–404.

29 Peter Stansky, *Redesigning the World: William Morris, the 1880s, and the Arts and Crafts* (Princeton, 1985).

30 Exhibitions of this style, such as Wendy Kaplan, *The Art that Is Life: The Arts and Crafts Movement in America*, exh. cat., Museum of Fine Arts (Boston, 1987) or Robert Judson Clark, *The Arts and Crafts Movement in America 1876–1916*, exh. cat., The Art Museum, Princeton University (Princeton, 1972).

4

The principles of the XIIth and XIIIth centuries are right in design, composition, colour combination and decorative effects.

Ralph Adams Cram, *Letter to William Willet*, 1912[1]

Before the ascendancy of Modernism of the 1950s, inspiration from historical periods such as the Middle Ages or the Italian Renaissance was standard for work in architecture as well as stained glass. America had early experienced Gothic revival in the mid-nineteenth century and saw a resurgence of this style for churches between 1915 and 1950 – a second Gothic Revival. This was rooted in economic expansion supporting this new wave of stylistic change. The early twentieth century saw the construction of many churches and new buildings that began filling America's growing suburban areas. In addition to new construction, many existing churches were replacing windows with new ones in the Second Gothic Revival Style. Common justifications for commissioning new windows included replacing non-figural windows installed at the time the church was built that were seen as temporary. Also churches replaced earlier windows that were now perceived as out of date.[2] Books such as John Gilbert Lloyd's *Stained Glass in America* or Charles J. Connick's *Adventures in Light and Color* argued that modern stained glass windows were viable only when based on "true principles" of glazing as demonstrated by windows of the cathedral of Chartres (figures 34, 35) or the Sainte-Chapelle of Paris.[3]

Nineteenth Century Precedent

As discussed in the previous chapter, inspiration from the French Gothic – red and blue color harmonies in small medallion scenes devoid of three-dimensional representation – had already been introduced into American buildings in the mid-nineteenth century. In 1849, St. James the Less in Philadelphia, a faithful replication of a "country church" in the early thirteenth-century English style, placed a *Tree of Jesse* in the French "archaeological" mode above the altar.[4] In the nineteenth-century revival of glass in France, architects distinguished between the "archaeological" mode that closely adhered to twelfth and thirteenth-century styles and the *vitrail-tableau* that incorporated later three-dimensional characteristics.[5] For the St. James the Less windows, which received high praise from Ecclesiologist circles in England and New York, Alfred Gérente, a glass painter/fabricator in Paris, closely emulated thirteenth-century models, setting stylized medieval figures against a flat blue background.[6]

By the turn of the century, however, both commercial and Arts and Crafts studios were producing windows more inspired by art of the later Middle Ages. Charles Eamer Kempe (1834–1907) of London, for instance, had established a thriving studio responsible for many commissions in the United States, such as the great *Jesse Tree* in the Church of the Advent, Boston, (1897), and the windows of several chapels of St. John the Divine, New York City (1916 and 1918).[7] Kempe's style evoked fifteenth-century glazing and panel-painting traditions, exemplified by the *Creed Window* from Hampton Court, now in the Museum of Fine Arts,

FIGURE 34
Cathedral of Chartres
*The Second Coming
of Christ, c. 1220*
South Rose

FIGURE 35
Cathedral of Chartres
*Head of the Prophet
Daniel* (detail), 1205–15
South nave, bay 141

FIGURE 36

Artist unknown

*Gothic Revival
Patterned Window,*
1930s

Conrad Schmitt Studios,
New Berlin, WI

FIGURE 37
Artist unknown
*Traditional Floral
Patterned Window,*
1880–1930
Collection Conrad
Schmitt Studios,
New Berlin, WI

Boston. English windows of the fifteenth century are characterized by their adherence to the Perpendicular style. Figures in vibrant color, set against white glass backgrounds, are framed by architectural canopies also made of deeply saturated colored glass. The art of Christopher Whall and the Arts and Crafts movement, discussed in the previous chapter, also found inspiration in the late medieval styles, seen in their juxtaposition of large amounts of uncolored glass with segments of color and silverstain yellows.

Two ornamental windows in this exhibition exemplify the difference in inspiration based on late or early-medieval models. The *Traditional Floral Patterned Window* panel (figure 37) shows a pattern of circles of predominantly uncolored glass detailed by neutral trace paint and silver stain (silver solution applied to glass that turns yellow upon firing) set within narrow borders. It is based on models like

York Minster's Chapter House and other English windows from around 1300.[8] The curving ornament retains something of late nineteenth century Victorian stylized floral decoration so prevalent in opalescent windows discussed earlier. The dynamism of the work is achieved in part by the skillful application of matte paint that creates shifting intensity of light within silver and gold harmonies. In contrast, the *Gothic Revival Patterned Window* (figure 36) emulates twelfth-and early thirteenth-century patterns of border ornament from the windows of Canterbury Cathedral.

Carefully crafted windows that closely emulated medieval precedents were possible because the American Gothic Revival studios, like their European predecessors, could rely on publications by restorers of stained glass. Many restorers published books with lavish reproductions and tracings or

FIGURE 38
**Charles J. Connick
(1875–1945)**

*Coronation of the
Virgin*, late 1920s

Boston Public Library,
Boston, MA

FIGURE 39

**Charles J. Connick
(1875–1945)**

*Coronation of
the Virgin* (detail),
late 1920s

Boston Public Library,
Boston, MA

other detailed restoration drawings. As discussed in chapter one, Westlake's *History of Design in Stained Glass*, for instance, was an essential reference for American studios. Translations of Viollet-le-Duc's section on stained glass from his *Dictionnaire* (1854–68) were also available. Indeed, many of the illustrations that Connick used for his own work, *Adventures in Light and Color*, were borrowed from the books of Westlake and Viollet-le-Duc. Like the works of Westlake and Viollet-le-Duc, Hugh Arnold (1872–1915) and Lawrence Saint's (1885–1961) *Stained Glass of the Middle Ages in England and France* was cherished by glass studios for its clear overview of what had become the canon of great medieval windows: Le Mans, Poitiers, Canterbury, Chartres, York, through Rouen and Fairford of the fifteenth century.[9] That medieval windows were valued above all other glass, however, had everything to do with the taste of collectors and writers.

Twelfth and Thirteenth Century Stylistic Dominance

Writers such as Henry Adams (1838–1918), with his influential book *Mont-Saint-Michel and Chartres*, prioritized the twelfth and thirteenth centuries as ideal moments in world history. In 1906, Adams advised Isabella Stewart Gardner (1840–1924), a Boston Brahmin and avid art collector, to purchase a large stained glass window from Soissons Cathedral, Soissons, France, now dated between 1195 and 1210–15, and installed it in the chapel of her Fenway mansion.[10] Adams believed the window came from the twelfth-century abbey church of Saint-Denis, not a surprising assumption given his knowledge of the dismantling of the abbey's windows in the early nineteenth century and the ensuing confusion over their provenance. The value of Adam's pioneering influence is attested by the 1913 re-edition of *Mont-Saint-Michel and Chartres* that included an introduction by the influential architect Ralph Adams Cram.[11] He praised Adams for perceiving

the unity of art, philosophy, politics, economics, and religion in "the greatest epoch of Christian civilization."[12] Thus the adaptation, or collecting, of the early Gothic style would be a means of restoring the values of Christianity at its height. Twelfth and thirteenth-century windows, either as museum objects or as models for new work, took priority in the United States.

By the late 1920s, as demonstrated by the circular medallion presenting the *Coronation of the Virgin* (figures 38, 39) designed by Charles J. Connick, artists looked to the medieval precedents of both the twelfth-century Romanesque style typified by windows in Le Mans cathedral (figure 40) and thirteenth-century Gothic style exemplified by the windows in the Sainte-Chapelle, Paris. The dominant color of the windows is blue with off-whites and yellows. The red of the background, warmer towards the center, is balanced by areas of dark wash selectively lightened with short strokes of the stylus to remove the matte paint. In keeping with the medieval figural aesthetic, modeling of Christ and the Virgin's faces is limited to several tonal values and dark trace outlines, as was recommended in the twelfth-century treatise of Theophilus, *On Diverse Arts*, a handbook for the applied arts of the Middle Ages.[13] The glass that Connick chose is thick, showing an undulating surface that enhances the variety of light refracted through it. Connick worked in this Second Gothic Revival style after 1925. As discussed in chapter three, up until this time, Connick's work had been deeply influenced by the Arts and Crafts style and the work of Christopher Whall.

Ongoing Challenges

The polemics surrounding the choice of Gothic style over other historic styles appear linked to competition for clients in the marketplace. The Second Gothic Revival style was but one of many styles in which stained glass windows were made during the first two decades of the twentieth

FIGURE 40

Ascension Window
(detail), 1140–1145,
Bay XVI,

Cathedral of Le Mans,
Le Mans, France

The Munich Studio

FIGURE 41

**The Munich Studio
(1901–1932), Chicago, IL**

Angel, c. 1910

Collection Conrad
Schmitt Studios,
New Berlin, WI

century. Between 1905 and 1925 the opalescent style was widely popular. At this time, the United States was also importing a great deal of work from English Victorian studios and German and Austrian studios that made windows like the *Angel* from The Munich Studio of Chicago, Illinois (figure 41). The figural model for such windows is derived from Italian Renaissance paintings of the kind that had earlier inspired the Nazarene movement, without question the most significant influence for German nineteenth-century glass.[14] Johann Friedrich Overbeck (1789–1869) set the Nazarene movement's initial philosophy by founding a "Brotherhood of St. Luke" and moving with followers into a secularized monastery on the outskirts of Rome in 1810. Artists in fresco, easel painting, and stained glass produced images melding Catholic religious feeling with a Raphaelesque air of idealism; they favored glowing colors, Renaissance figural types, and smoothly detailed surfaces – characteristics that translated perfectly into stained glass figural windows such as those installed in the nave of Cologne cathedral in the 1840s.[15]

With the rise of purchasing power by Catholic congregations around the turn of the nineteenth century, imports from the Catholic areas of Bavaria and Austria had inundated the American market. The city of Munich had long been viewed as the premier example of the revival of liturgical arts under an inspired monarch, Ludwig I of Bavaria (1786–1868), and Catholics were convinced of the importance of the glass as a testimony to the validity of their faith. Studios like Von Gerichten of Columbus, Ohio (1893–1937),[16] Emil Frei of St. Louis (f. 1900), and The Munich Studio, as well as others catered to this taste by producing stained glass windows that illustrated figures set in three-dimensional pictorial space that were heavily painted in realistic detail right here at home in the United States.

Antipathy for both opalescent and Munich style windows was profound in Gothic Revival circles. Ralph Adams Cram, a major Gothic Revival proponent, characterized opalescent windows as inappropriate for a spiritual atmosphere and gave explicit directions to studios to avoid them. His disdain for opalescent glass may very well have been associated with its ubiquity. Its very presence in lampshades, row-house stairwells, or public theaters convinced Cram of its inappropriateness for the church. It bears repeating that Cram's efforts began the twentieth-century polarization that relegated the stained glass window to church decoration. The split between stained glass as a fine art and stained glass as a religious expression remained until the 1960s when a rebirth of stained glass became again linked to contemporaneous work in painting and manufactured objects.

Cram was also explicit in his criticism of Munich style windows. Writing for *Stained Glass* in 1931, he stated that they were "too terrible to contemplate" and argued that it had become a question of "how to get rid of them without impiety. There was and is but one way. Go they must …" Cram called for replacement windows of the same subject "but made by real artists," flattering the stained glass trade perhaps in an attempt to realize his agenda. Cram's edict was followed. For example, windows in the chancel of the Cathedral of the Holy Cross, Boston, depicting the Passion of Christ, produced in 1875, were replaced in the 1950s by non figural blue windows by the O'Duggan Studio, Boston.

Growth of the Gothic Revival

Many American studios, sensing the growing architectural bias towards the early Gothic, espoused its style perhaps in an effort to maintain regular commissions. Since architects favoring the Gothic Revival style often played a role in selecting a stained glass studio, the trend favoring the Gothic style soon became almost universal. A cursory examination of the commissions of studios in business since the

beginning of the twentieth century shows the shift from opalescent windows to some variation of Gothic Revival. The Emil Frei studio of St. Louis, specializing in antique figural windows in the Munich style, was producing by 1930 windows in unmitigated Gothic Revival patterns, as can be seen in the Second Presbyterian Church of St. Louis.[17] The Henry Keck (1913–1974) studio of Syracuse, New York, originally working in opalescent style, was working in the Second Gothic Revival style by the 1920s.[18] English born Clement Heaton (1861–1940) came to the United Sates in 1915 as a mature artist at the behest of Ralph Adams Cram. Heaton designed Art Nouveau work around 1905 and was producing French-inspired Gothic Revival windows by 1920, as seen in the west rose of the Church of the Blessed Sacrament in New York.[19]

Jewish as well as Christian congregations espoused the Gothic Revival. By the 1920s, American architects and stained glass designers had accepted the Gothic as a style uniquely suitable for the material of glass. Whether set in elaborate Gothic Revival buildings or decorating a more modest edifice, the window itself seemed to breathe spirituality simply by evoking a medieval age of faith. A brilliant example in this exhibition is the *Border with Menorah* panel. It shows dense a medallion style construction with small segments of glass, arranged in strong red and blue contrasts (figure 42).

William Willet (1869–1921) of Philadelphia, was considered an early force in the Second Gothic Revival, a man responsible for the West Point chapel (dedicated 1910) and the *Seven Liberal Arts* window of the Graduate School, at Princeton University.[20] Nicola d'Ascenzo (1871–1954), also of Philadelphia, produced varied works based on medieval inspiration such as the Washington Memorial Chapel, Valley Forge, Pennsylvania, about 1915–24. Charles J. Connick of Boston, however, was the movement's chief polemicist, and owner of possibly its most prolific studio.

The popularity of the Second Gothic Revival architectural style in America coincided with the growth of American colleges and universities. Associated with the English precedents of the university complexes of Oxford and Cambridge, the Gothic mode found fertile ground in the American university expansion. Princeton, Yale, Boston College, and the Universities of Chicago and Michigan were some of the many schools engaged in complex building programs in the 1920s.[21] Admiration for authentic heraldic glass, displaying the arms of great families, such as that purchased by the prominent collector Edsel Ford,[22] was at the foundation of these contemporary new constructions on American campuses.

As families like the Morgans of the Gilded Age sought validity through collecting antique glass, prominent families in the 1920s endowed building campaigns that emphasized their own lineage. Heraldry, even imaginary, appealed because it used the brilliant patterns of Art Deco design and also because one could construct allusions of a medieval past without the taint of religious imagery in a secular setting. Revival styles incorporating heraldic shields or Swiss Renaissance panels were also popular, especially for library settings such as Yale University, where Owen Bonawit (1891–1971) executed glass for the architect William Gamble Rodgers.[23] At Boston College, Earl Sanborn (1890–1937) glazed the Bapst Library for architects Maginnis and Walsh, Boston; and at Princeton University, Charles Connick and William Willet, among others, installed glass for the buildings designed by Ralph Adams Cram.[24]

Boston in particular, it seems, saw the rise of large and influential Gothic Revival stained glass studios such as those of Charles Connick, Wilbur Herbert Burnham, Joseph G. Reynolds, Francis & J. H. Rohnstock; Walter C. Ball, Earl Edward Sanborn, and Margaret Redmond (1867–1948).[25] The imagery selected by the Second Gothic Revival artists contrasts markedly with that of the nineteenth century, whether traditional European or American opalescent. The Gothic design most often favored small medallions set against mosaic grounds similar to those in the glass from the cathedral of Chartres, the Sainte-Chapelle or other High Gothic examples. The interest in Gothic style glass reflected interests of scholars in the history of the Middle Ages. Ralph Adams Cram, for example, was one of the founding members of the Medieval Academy of America and Connick's vast library of medieval sources brought Gothic Revival subjects and style to an audience in virtually every part of America.

One of the more promising members of the stained glass craft, however, never lived to see the full realization of his talent. Harry Wright Goodhue (1905–31) was the son of the glass designer Harry Eldredge Goodhue and nephew of Bertram Goodhue, a partner in the firm of Cram, Goodhue and Ferguson. Wright Goodhue showed a precocious ability as a teen to fuse revival and contemporary styles. His work showed a progressive adaptation of the abstract tendencies of twentieth-century art. His works include the rose windows of the chancel and transepts of the Church of the Sacred Heart, Jersey City, New Jersey and windows of the crossing and choir clerestory, Princeton University Chapel.[26] Wright Goodhue's windows often display bold graphic simplicity, emphasizing rhythmic sweeps of curving line, not too far removed from the American painter, Arthur Dove's (1880–1946) earlier abstractions such as *Nature Symbolized No 2*, 1911, now at the Art Institute of Chicago. Wright Goodhue also produced sculpture that was very contemporary and close to the organic forms of the American John B. Flannagan (1895–1942).[27]

The application of medieval styles in the Second Gothic Revival was extremely widespread and continued well into the 1950s. The reasons for the style's long life were varied. Often windows were commissioned over time resulting in Gothic Revival style windows dating to various decades made for a church. In addition, congregations also chose studios and an artistic style with which they were familiar. These factors resulted in the partiality shown by congregations to the Gothic Revival window.

At the same time many congregations were committed to an imagery that recalled their traditions. For example, Orthodox churches were keenly sensitive to the painted icon tradition with its medieval two-dimensionality and noble power. A saint's dress and pose remained symbolic throughout the centuries. The image of *St. George* (figure 43) fabricated by Franklin Art Glass Studios, Columbus, Ohio, (1950s?) demonstrates how glass can easily adapt to such requirements. The main figure of St. George is posed facing front dressed in traditional armor. The face, an elongated oval with large limpid eyes, recalls Greek icon painting of the Middle Ages. The bright colors and flat background enhance the timeless nature of the saint's presence.

In contrast, *Christ in the Garden of Gethsemane* (figure 44), dating from the 1950s, a demonstration piece (a sample window made by a studio to illustrate their work), profiles the narrative qualities of the Gothic style for religious programs. The figure is in action and we can identify a specific event in Christ's life. Unlike Connick's *Coronation of the Virgin* from the late 1920s (figure 38) *Christ in the Garden of Gethsemane* is less bound to a specific medieval prototype. The image of Christ is not set in a medallion pattern but rather enmeshed into an abstract geometric pattern characteristic of Art Deco influence which encouraged greater linear qualities in draftsmanship.

As mentioned above, because of the availability of printed accurate tracings of medieval windows published by nineteenth-century restorers, the twentieth-century studio was able to base its Second Gothic Revival work on authoritative sources for styles and iconography. The printed illustrations emphasized the abstract and graphic nature of stained glass painting. A leaded stained glass window created exactly that section of "translucent wall, richly decorated" praised by Gothic Revival architects like Cram.[28] During the early part of the twentieth century, the tendencies in American art toward greater abstraction and bold contrasts, and the subsequent Art Deco movement, corresponded to the emphasis on graphic intensity prized by the Gothic revival. For even when an historic style is being emulated, it is invariably filtered through the artist's contemporary aesthetic.

FIGURE 43
Artist unknown
St. George, 1950s?
Collection Franklin
Art Glass, Columbus, OH

FIGURE 44
Artist unknown
Christ in the Garden of Gethsemane, 1950s?
Collection Franklin
Art Glass, Columbus, OH

ENDNOTES

1 Ralph Adams Cram, Letter to Willliam Willet, 1912, courtesy Helene Weis.

2 Catholic churches were frequently constructed in two stages. The first saw the structure completed and usually the embellishment of the sanctuary. When this debt was retired, another campaign inserted pictorial windows throughout the edifice. Older more affluent congregations were often prone to replace existing windows, even with figural images.

3 John Gilbert Lloyd, *Stained Glass in America* (Jenkintown, 1963) and Charles Connick, *Adventures in Light and Color* (New York, 1937).

4 *Ecclesiologist* 9 (April, 1849), 351; Phoebe Stanton, *The Gothic Revival and American Church Architecture: An Episode of Taste, 1840–1856* (Baltimore/London, 1968), 106–107.

5 Catherine Brisac and Didier Alliou, "La peinture sur verre au XIXe siècle dans la Sarthe," *Annales de Bretagne et des Pays de l'Ouest* (1986): 389–93, figs. 13–14. The entire issue studies nineteenth-century stained glass. See also *Vitrea, Revue du Centre International du Vitrail*, Chartres, 3/1 (1989); *Etudes Normandes*, Association d'Etudes Normandes 4 (1989); Chantal Bouchon et al., *Ces Eglises du dix-neuvième siècle* (Amiens, 1993); *Le Vitrail au XIXe siècle et les ateliers manceaux*, exh. cat., Musée du Mans (Le Mans, 1998); Virginia Raguin, "Revivals, Revivalists, and Architectural Stained Glass," *Journal of the Society of Architectural Historians* 49/3 (1990), 310–329.

6 A society dedicated to the reform of church worship and architecture was founded in 1839 as the Cambridge Camden Society in Cambridge, England. In 1845 it moved to London, becoming the Ecclesiological Society. Under the direction of Benjamin Webb, John Mason Neale, and Alexander Beresford-Hope, the Society exerted a major influence on church architecture. Its journal, *The Ecclesiologist*, published between 1841 and 1868, included both scholarly articles and criticism.

7 Margaret Stavridi, *Master of Glass: Charles Eamer Kempe 1837–1907* (Hatfield, 1988).

8 Richard Marks, *Stained Glass in England* (Toronto, 1993), figs. 117, 121.

9 Hugh Arnold/Lawrence Saint, *Stained Glass of the Middle Ages in England and France* (London, 1913); also Lawrence Saint, "Is Stained Glass a Lost Art," *Bulletin of the American Ceramic Society* 15/11 (1936), 375–82. Saint is explicit about his admiration for the twelfth century art of France, citing Chartres' west windows and cathedral of Poitiers's crucifixion as "the greatest windows in the world." See also Virginia Raguin, "Lawrence Saint and the North Rose of Washington Cathedral," *Stained Glass* 78/3 (Fall 1983), 236–37, and Robin Hathaway Keisman, "Working with Lawrence Saint: An Interview with John Hathaway," Ibid., 238–42.

10 Harold Dean Cater, *Henry Adams and his Friends: A Collection of his Unpublished Letters* (Boston, 1947), 584–87.

11 Douglass Shand-Tucci, *Ralph Adams Cram: Life and Architecture*, vol. 1, *Boston Bohemia* (Amherst, 1995).

12 Henry Adams, *Mont-Saint-Michel and Chartres* (Princeton, 1981), V.

13 Theophilus, *On Divers Arts: The Treatise of Theophilus*, ed. John G. Hawthorne and Cyril Stanley Smith (Chicago, 1963).

14 Keith Andrews, *The Nazarenes: A Brotherhood of German Painters in Rome* (New York, 1988); Michael Caffort, "Les Nazaréens français," in *Le Vitrail au XIXe siècle et les ateliers manceaux*, exh. cat., Musée du Mans, (Le Mans, 1998), 39–67; William Vaughn, *German Romanticism in English Art* (London, 1980). For early German glass see Elgin Vaassen, *Bilder auf Glas: Glasgemälde zwischen 1780 und 1870* (Munich, 1997).

15 *Glasmalerei des 19. Jahrhunderts*, exh. cat., Angermuseum, Erfurt (Leipzig, 1993), 24, 122–25, nos. 36–37. For superb illustration of the Lamentation window see Arnold Wolff, *The Cologne Cathedral* (Cologne, 1990), fig. 76.

16 Craig T. Walley, "Deeds of Light: Von Gerichten Art Glass," *Timeline*, Ohio Historical Society 15 (August 1998), 26–41; Dennis Shobe and Jonathan Brown, "Light … After Forty Years of Darkness," *Stained Glass* 73 (Fall 1978), 183–88; Helene Weis, "The Enigmatic Von Gerichtens," Ibid., 91 (Fall 1996), 282–89.

17 See for overview: Mary M. Stiritz, *St Louis: Historic Churches & Synagogues* (St. Louis, 1995).

18 Cleota Reed, ed., *Henry Keck Stained Glass Studio 1913–1974* (Syracuse, 1985).

19 Nicole Quellet-Soguel/Walter Tschopp, eds., *Clement Heaton, 1861–1940 Londres - Neuchatel - New York* (Hauterive, 1996), 26–27, 60–61.

20 Virginia Raguin, *Glory in Glass*, 130–32.

21 See especially, the Michigan Law Triangle, Ilene H. Forsyth, *The Uses of Art: Medieval Metaphor in the Michigan Law Quadrangle* (Ann Arbor, 1993).

22 Installed in the Edsel and Eleanor Ford House, Grosse Pointe Shores, Michigan. Virginia Raguin/Helen Zakin, *Stained Glass before 1700 in the Collections of the Midwest States, Corpus Vitrearum, United States of America*, VIII/2 (London, 2001), 91–116.

23 Gay Walker, *Bonawit, Stained Glass & Yale* (Wilsonville, 2000).

24 Richard Stillwell, *The Chapel of Princeton University* (Princeton, 1971).

25 See Connick, *Adventures in Light and Color*, esp. 349–77, 400–4, 408, for information on these studios and location of many of their works. A sampling of Gothic Revival worked by Wilbur H. Burnham, Earl Edward Sanborn, Joseph G. Reynolds, Lawrence B. Saint and others is found in Nancy S. Montgomery/Marcia P. Johnson, eds., *Jewels of Light. The Stained Glass and Mosaics of Washington Cathedral*, (Washington, D.C., 1984). For the Burnham studio see Norman Temme, "The Burnhams: A Story of Outstanding Achievement," *Stained Glass* 77 (Winter/Spring 1983), 366–70. For a personal statement very similar those by Connick and Lawrence Saint see Wilbur Herbert Burnham, "Stained Glass Construction and Details," *Architectural Forum* 40 (1924), 1–10.

26 Richard Stillwell, *The Chapel of Princeton University* (Princeton, 1971), 36–39; see also apse window of Mercersburg Academy Chapel, Mercersburg, Pennsylvania (communication from Jay L. Quinn, Alumni Secretary); Church of the Holy Rosary, Pittsburgh, Pennsylvania; and south clerestory window of Emmanuel Church, Newport, Rhode Island. Ralph Adams Cram wrote a moving tribute to the artist: "Personal Recollections of Harry Wright Goodhue," *Stained Glass* 27 (1932), 263–73, which includes discussion and illustrations of other commissions as well. See also obituary, Ibid, 26 (September 1931), 311–13.

27 See illustration in article "Fogg Museum Honors Goodhue's Memory," *Boston Evening Transcript* (March 26, 1932).

28 Letter from Cram to William Willet, June 28, 1912, courtesy Helene Weis.

THE LAST FIFTY YEARS

The United States [is] a fantastic giant in its openness, a country that is dynamic, creative, eager and rich in experiences.

Benoit Gilsoul, *Stained Glass* 80, Fall 1985[1]

Since the 1950s, the stained glass artist has become less and less focused on the design of "a window" and "more and more in the simultaneous creation of a light-filled architectural unit."[2] The stained glass designer moved more closely to a relationship with contemporary fine arts, paying special attention to color field, abstract expressionism, and minimalism. Contemporary architectural glass has also been influenced by the rise of interest in glass as a sculptural material. The growth of the "hot glass" movement in particular has encouraged experimentation with materials and effects that had been incorporated in the "flat" (window) movement.

Throughout the history of stained glass, its finest moments of creativity have always been linked to similar expressions in other media. For instance, the unmodulated use of color, graphic intensity of line, and insistent planar construction of the twelfth century was precisely that of contemporaneous manuscript illumination and wall painting. In the nineteenth-century revival of stained glass, William Morris's work in glass was associated with the painting of the Pre-Raphaelites. In the twentieth century, artists associated with German Modernist movements radically transformed stained glass, linking contemporary painting to window design and exerting a profound influence on American production.

Germany suffered massive material loss as a result of World War II, during which many churches were destroyed or severely damaged. In the *Wirtschaftswunder* (economic miracle) of recovery,

concerted efforts to rebuild and rededicate churches increased opportunities for artists working with glass. Post World War II German glass artists were at the forefront of aesthetic innovation.

Robert Sowers was key to bringing the work of German glass artists in the wake of World War II to a wider audience. Ludwig Schaffrath (1924–), the most influential personality of the movement, credits Sowers as the first American to discover the "new German glass." Sowers's book *The Lost Art* made a deep impact on American artists, encouraging an entire generation to "make the pilgrimage to Germany – in the truest sense of the expression – to see these works."[3] Sowers did not prioritize the work of artists in one country. In *The Lost Art* he gave considerable attention to progressive artists of many nationalities: French (Jean Barillet and Henri Matisse (1869–1954)), Irish (Evie Hone (1894–1955)), German (Georg Meistermann (1911–)) and Dutch (Joep Nicolas (1897–1971)). To Sowers, the universal concern in the construction of stained glass was radiance and graphic structure, which he saw expressed most in contemporary German work.

In Sowers's most comprehensive book entitled *Language of Stained Glass,* 51 of the 118 images of stained glass windows reflect works of the German Modernism. An example of the art that moved Sowers is found in a window by Johannes Schreiter (1930–) made for the Grunewaldkirche, Berlin (figure 45). Schreiter, who was a vital part of conferences such as Portcon in Palo Alto, California,

FIGURE 45

**Johannes Schreiter
(1930–)**

Model window panels

Grunewaldkirche,
Berlin, 2001

Collection Derix Glasstudios,
Taunusstein, Germany

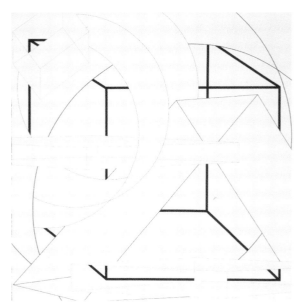

FIGURE 46
Al Held (1928–)
Jupiter V, 1974
Acrylic on canvas
Museum of Fine Arts,
Boston, MA

pioneered the use of lead as a design graphic. Rather than function simply as a connective element and divider between colors, the leads become independent lines intersecting the fields created by the expanses of color.

Stained glass, long considered an artistic expression that crossed borders, began in the 1950s to see collaboration among designers and fabricators across national boundaries, in the process bringing German progressive art to the United States. Artists began moving among countries to study and apprentice themselves to studios. The Pilchuck School, for instance, in Washington, welcomed international artists to the United States.[4] Founded in 1971, the school continues to foster creative exchange among practicing artists and aspiring students of hot and flat (window) glass. The Pilchuck school has become a key resource for developing progressive work in the last quarter of the twentieth century.

The tendency since the 1950s to abstract imagery in stained glass was also part of the general direction of contemporary art in America. Parallels among artists are evoked by Frank Stella's (1936–)

protractor series of brilliant color and texture, Robert Motherwell's (1915–1991) large floating forms, and Brigit Riley's (1931–) abstracted colored light. Al Held's (1928–) subdued interactions parallel one of *Reflections on Glass's* featured artists, David Wilson, who achieves a marvelous play of geometry and a subtle shift of intensity through textures of uncolored glass. In *Jupiter V* (figure 46), Held restricts the canvas to black and white.[5] A few thin lines (which could almost be leads) intersect, yet create the impression of immensely complicated space. Other, more gestural expressions, such as that of Willem De Kooning's (1904–1997) energetic brushstrokes, parallel the use of paint by Ellen Mandelbaum, an artist also featured in the exhibition.

In painting, too, changes developed, particularly with color field works where their power was connected to their large size. The sheer size of a color field painting could create a "field" that could exert a physical force on the spectator similar to the one evoked by an architectural presence. One of the purest examples of large scale color field painting is the Rothko Chapel installation (figure 47), part of

FIGURE 47

**Marc Rothko
(1903–1970)**

Rothko Chapel (interior view), 1971

Menil Collection,
Houston, TX

the Menil collection in Houston, Texas.[6] Opened in 1971, the chapel was conceived with three elements in mind: an octagonal brick church, Marc Rothko's (1903–1970) paintings, and Barnett Newman's (1905–1970) *Broken Obelisk* dedicated to Martin Luther King, Jr., set in a reflecting pool facing the chapel. Rigorously aniconic, the paintings' message is developed by the spatial presence of deep color set within subtly varied rectangles. The chapel operates in a manner similar to installations of glass where the light, with or without recognizable image, permeates an interior. Modern glazing often produces a sensation of depth using vibrant color that advances and recedes and seems to hover in space according to the intensity of the light permeating it. The concept of color penetrating space is often seen as analogous to the resonance of musical tone. The chapel, stressing meditation, is one of the most uncompromising sacred spaces. Indeed, the Rothko chapel has been the site of international conferences on music and on spirituality, especially meditation.

The mid-century brought heightened collaboration between the architect, new materials and new processes. One of the first new techniques

was *dalle-de-verre*, an innovation pioneered in the United States by the immigration of French artists Robert Pinart and Jean-Jacques Duval. French commissions on American soil, however, were also substantial. Gabriel Loire (1904–1996), head of a large French studio in the village of Levres, two kilometers from Chartres, designed several important American installations.[7] Loire's seminal work for America was his First Presbyterian Church, Stanford, Connecticut, built 1956–57. Great concrete ribs arch upwards within a fish-like structure to house Loire's glass. The technique can also be seen in the *Virgin and Child* (figure 48), created in 1961 by Carl Huneke of San Francisco, a work in which the central image is sculpted with abstract chunks of glass, but the delicacy of the young mother and infant is still communicated.

The use of kiln-formed or molded glass – as described in chapter six – is a direct offshoot of sculptural techniques. Major artists in the leaded glass field, such as Lutz Haufschild (1943–), a Canadian with many ties to the United States, also saw its potential. Haufschild designed windows for the Sports Dome, Ontario in 1987. His naturalistic

FIGURE 48
**Carl Huneke
(1898–1972)**

Virgin and Child, **1961**

**Fabricated by Century
Stained Glass Studio,
San Francisco, CA**

Collection
Terry Blaine

sports figures depicted in action achieve an abstract presence through the silver tones of uncolored glass cast with relief images.[8] Douglas Hansen (1949–), represented in this exhibition by his kiln-formed windows for the Saint Ignatius Chapel, produced a glass wall inspired by Japanese painting of Koi fish for the Keiro Nursing Home in Seattle, Washington in 1986,[9] and Stephen Knapp, also one of our featured artists, has produced a kiln-formed panel for this exhibition.

A marked direction in stained glass was the entrance of already established artists. Clients and patrons alike became confident that the technical expertise was becoming available to allow collaboration of the most creative designers and fabricators. This direction parallels similar collaborative work of contemporary artists and "fabricating" printmaking studios such as that of Tatyana Grosman's Universal Limited Art Editions studio in West Islip, New York, which collaborated with Robert Rauschenberg (1925–), among many others, in pioneering the modern print revival.[10] Creative, personal expression, as known in the medium of painting, was reclaimed for the domain of printmaking. In England the painter John Piper (1903–1992) entered the field of glass with an initial association with Patrick Reyntians (1925–) who taught in 1977, 1981, and 2002 at the Pilchuck school. In the United States, Georgy Kepes (1906–2001), professor of Visual Arts at the Massachusetts Institute of Technology (MIT), Boston, began to design in glass, including a *dalle-de-verre* mural for the KLM Airline Ticket Office in Manhattan and a similar installation at the Harvard Square transit station in Cambridge, Massachusetts. Kepes's best-known ecclesiastical commissions are the towering windows in *dalle-de-verre* (symbolizing the four elements) for St. Mary's Cathedral, San Francisco. A recent example of collaborative process can be seen in Patrick Heron's (1920–) work commissioned in 1994 for installation in the Tate Gallery St. Ives, Cornwall, England.[11] His large window

design, reminiscent of the simple floating shapes of dense color of Joan Miró, was executed by the Derix Glasstudios, Taunusstein, Germany. Collaboration with the studio helped the designer explore methods that correspond to the artist's imagination. Heron's concepts were fabricated in a laminated technique to avoid use of lead, and the resulting windows were installed as two elements despite their size (over fifteen feet tall).

The collaboration of painter and glass fabricator is perhaps best exemplified in the work of Russian-born painter Marc Chagall (1887–1958). Chagall, an exponent of painterly abstraction, lived most of his life in France, but spent the years from 1941 until 1947 in the United States. One of his most famous projects is the ceiling of the Metropolitan Opera house at Lincoln Center in New York City. The artist designed his first series of windows in 1954. These were a series installed in the baptistery of the Church of Notre-Dame-de-Toute-Grâce at Plateau d'Assy, already graced with windows by the painters Georges Rouault (1871–1958) and Jean Bazaine (1904–). Subsequently, Chagall began an ongoing collaboration with the craftsman Charles Marq (1923–) to produce many windows installed in prestigious locations; two such examples are the renowned "Jerusalem" windows for the Synagogue of the Hadassah-Hebrew University Medical Center in Jerusalem (1960–1962)[12] and the windows he designed in 1964 for the Union Church, Pocantico Hills, New York, a memorial for John D. Rockefeller (figure 49).[13]

Currently, the contemporary art world is witnessing a return to figural imagery. For example, Robert Rauschenberg continues to produce compelling works mixing the realism of photography and the intense experience of the gestural brushstroke that emphasizes the picture plane. David Hockney (1937–) moves easily among poster-like hard edges and a more gestural form. Large meditative space, as discussed for the Rothko Chapel,

FIGURE 49
**Marc Chagall
(1887–1985)**

Good Samaritan, 1964

The Union Church
of Pocantico Hills, NY

Memorial for John D.
Rockefeller

FIGURE 50

Arthur Stern (1950–)
Randy Dixon

Station of the Cross
(detail), 1987

St. Mary's Parish,
Lakeport, CA

can also feature the image, as seen in the Ascension Mausoleum in Ramsey, New Jersey, the work of Ellen Miret, one of our featured artists.

In the realm of stained glass vehement polemics concerning representation are nothing new. The second Gothic Revival movement condemned the three-dimensionality of the opalescent "picture window" while in the 1950s Sowers, although criticizing most products of the Gothic Revival as uninspired, also saw illusionism as repugnant.[14] Artists like Albinas Elskus, however, have worked in a photo-realist style that could still be compatible with glass. Arthur Stern (1950–) Studios developed a series of *Stations of the Cross* for St. Mary's Parish Church in Lakeport, California, (figure 50) combining rectangular lattice and realistic black and white "snapshots" of Christ's journey drawn by Randy Dixon, an architect and religious illustrator.[15] Combining leaded with beveled and engraved glass, Stern's work evokes the geometric precision and transparency of Frank Lloyd Wright's style. In the history of glass, there have been as many different kinds of windows as there have been art movements – some monumental, some intimate in scale. One thing remains consistent however: the success of the window is the result of the designer's ability to understand the materials and to respond to the context. Today work in stained glass is as varied as it ever was, as the work of the following artists demonstrates.

CONTEMPORARY GLASS ARTISTS

FIGURE 51

Katharine Lamb Tait

**Fabricated by
J & R Lamb Studios**

*My Covenant of Peace
I Give to You*, late 1940s

The Corning Museum
of Glass, Corning, NY

KATHARINE LAMB TAIT (1895–1981) was born into an artistic family. Her father, Charles Rollinson Lamb (1860–1942), was the head of the firm of J & R Lamb founded by her grandfather Joseph Lamb and his brother Richard in 1857. Her mother, Ella Condie Lamb (1862–1936), was a portrait painter and designer. Katharine studied at the National Academy of Design, the Art Students' League in New York and the Cooper Union Art School where she later taught the Decorative Design course for four years. She returned to the Lamb Studios where she worked with her brother, Ken Barre Lamb.

Lamb Tait's career was both extensive and innovative. For the Marine Corps Chapel at Camp Lejeune in North Carolina, she worked in a conservative English style using a realistic drafting technique and extensive silver stain. The ten stained glass windows installed in 1948 depict Old Testament archangels above illustrations of major events in Marine Corps history. In the windows' borders are scenes from wartime photographs taken by Marines.

My Covenant of Peace I Give to You, on display in the exhibition (figure 51) commemorates the hopes for peace with the founding of the United Nations in 1945. Based on John 14.27, Christ's assurance to his apostles, "my peace I give unto you," she presents Christ's figure bathed in the rays of the Holy Spirit. In the upper left, a rainbow descends upon an image of the arc on Mount Ararat, recalling God's covenant with Noah. The emphasis on linear patterns and sharp color contrasts shows the influence of Art Deco in stained glass design even into the 1940s.

BIBLIOGRAPHY Orin Skinner, "Women in Stained Glass," *Stained Glass* 36 (Spring 1941),18–20; David Adams, "The Last Stained Glass Lamb: Katharine Lamb Tait, 1895–1981," Ibid. 77 (Spring 1982), 41–45.

FIGURE 52

Hendrik Van de Burgt

Fabricated by
J & R Lamb Studios

The Sower, **1964**

Collection Donald
Samick, J & R Lamb
Studios

HENDRIK VAN DE BURGT (1913–) was born in Arnhem, Netherlands. He studied art and stained glass at the Kunst Oefing in Arnhem, from 1931 to 1937. He has worked for the J & R Lamb Studios since 1952 designing windows. His commissions include windows for the Sutton Place Synagogue, Sutton Place, New York City; St. Thomas Roman Catholic Church, Amboy Road, Staten Island; and the Mausoleum Chapel, Holy Resurrection Cemetery, Staten Island. Like Helen Hickman's work discussed below, Van de Burgt's work represents the tradition of flexibility of designing styles. In *The Sower*, 1964 (figure 52), on display in the exhibition, Van de Burgt shows an abstracted figural style, while retaining a clear image of a man to illustrate one of Christ's parables of sowing the "seed" of the Word of God on various types of ground (Matt. 13:1–23). In the Synagogue window from the 1970s, on display in the exhibition, the style is more abstract, devoid of figural imagery and pictorial space. Symbols, however, abound: the dove with olive branch, the broken chains, and the tablets of the commandments given to Moses. Both panels are demonstration pieces (sample windows made independent of a commission to illustrate the studio's work for prospective clients) for the Lamb Studios.

FIGURE 53

Benoit Gilsoul

***The Two Trumpets
of Silver**, 1972–73*

Sanctuary of the
Congregation of Beth-
T'fillah, Philadelphia, PA

BENOIT GILSOUL (1914–2000) was born in Naumur, Belgium. He was graduated in 1938 from the Académie Royale des Beaux Arts in Brussels. He distinguished himself in painting and drawing as well as mosaics and murals in Europe with over 50 solo shows in Belgium, France, and Luxembourg. In 1958, Gilsoul became president of the Association des Artistes Belges. In 1960 he had his first solo show in New York City, where he began working more extensively with stained glass, becoming an American citizen in 1967. He spoke of his art as an effort to "separate the visible from the invisible to give that dimension a tangible form." His deep understanding of traditional form and abstraction made him a potent force among younger designers. Windows of 1972/73 for the Congregation of Beth-T'fillah, Philadelphia, Pennsylvania (figure 53) show Gilsoul's breadth of scope and ability to combine figurative ideals and modern abstraction. His many works are well represented in the Metropolitan New York area: United Nations Interfaith Chapel (1963), St. John the Evangelist Church at 55th Street (1972), Emmanuel Lutheran Church, 88th Street, St. John's Friary, Capuchin Center; Supreme Court Chambers, Trenton, New Jersey, and the Temple Shalom, Somerville, New Jersey.

BIBLIOGRAPHY Helen Weis, "Benoit Gilsoul," *Stained Glass* 80 (Fall 1985), 244–49.

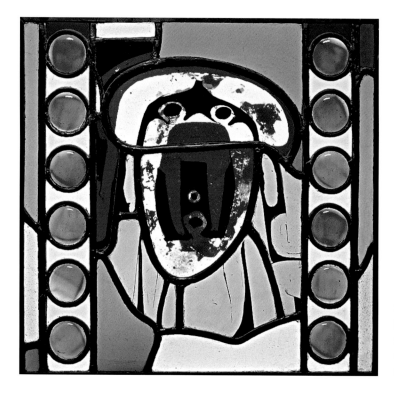

FIGURE 54
Robert Sowers
Red One, **1952**
The Corning Museum
of Glass, Corning, NY

ROBERT SOWERS (1923–1990) has been admired as the most influential American contemporary thinker in the field of glass, respected for both his art and his writing. He studied art at Florida Southern College before serving in the United States Army from 1943 through 1946. He subsequently received a BA from the New School for Social Research in New York and then his Masters from Columbia University in 1949. The primary catalyst for bringing the Modern German school to the attention of American artists, Sowers was awarded a Fulbright Fellowship in 1950 for travel to Europe, primarily England, to study the role of the visual arts in architecture. His panel *Red One* (figure 54), on display in the exhibition, was included in a show of *New Talent* at the Museum of Modern Art, New York City, in 1954 and illustrated in his book, *Stained Glass: An Architectural Art*. The head illustrated in *Red One* reflects Sower's study of medieval glass, in particular the design of large clerestory figures of prophets and apostles where the segment of the eyes and forehead is treated as one leaded unit and the lower portion of the face another.

BIBLIOGRAPHY See selected bibliography

FIGURE 55
Helen Carew Hickman
Pietà, 1952
The Corning Museum
of Glass, Corning, NY

HELEN CAREW HICKMAN (1925–) received her BFA in painting and design from Carnegie Mellon University in Pittsburgh in 1947. Upon graduation she spent a four-year apprenticeship at Hunt Stained Glass Studios in Pittsburgh, continuing as a designer through 1955. In 1951 she received the Studio Shop prize at the 41st Annual Associated Artists of Pittsburgh show for the *Pietà* (figure 55) now in the collection of the Corning Museum of Glass and on display in this exhibition. In 1952 her *Ascension* won the Designer-Craftsman Award. The *Pietà* shows her sensitivity to Modernist styles through abstraction of crucial elements to focus on the livid face of Christ pressed between his mother's hand and face. The Virgin's hand is linked with Christ's tortured hand through the diagonal and the coloration of his arm. The subtle balance of red against the dominant blues and purples shows the lingering influence of the "blue of Chartres," an ideal aesthetic for the Gothic Revival.

Hickman began work in 1961 for the Conrad Schmitt Studios, New Berlin, Wisconsin, later becoming their head designer, working with facility in both traditional and contemporary designs. In 1978, she became the first woman president of the Stained Glass Association of America.

BIBLIOGRAPHY Richard Millard, "Meet Artist Designer: Helen Carew Hickman," *Stained Glass* 77 (Spring 1982), 23–25. Patricia Robert, "An Artist of Many Facets," Ibid. 74 (Spring 1979): 36–37; "Associated Artists Award – And Two Helens," Ibid. 47 (Spring 1952), 14–15.

FIGURE 56

Albinas Elskus (1926-)

Fabricated by Rambusch Studios, NY

Three Marys at the Tomb (detail), 1985

Mausoleum of the Good Shepherd, St. Gertrude's Cemetery, Colonia, NJ

ALBINAS ELSKUS (1926–), the author of *The Art of Painting on Glass* (New York, 1980), is arguably the most admired painter on glass of his generation. Elskus studied art and architecture in Lithuania, Germany, and France before coming to the United States where he became acquainted with the early Arts and Crafts designers, such as John Gordon Guthrie (1874–1961). His numerous commissions have always been able to blend his extraordinary gifts of draftsmanship with the architectural requirements of the leaded window. His influence on other artists operated through his personality and work, but also through his many workshops, including those at the Parson's School of Design, New York, and the Pilchuck School of Glass, Stanwood, Washington, where he was an artist-in-residence. In the New York area his work is found at the Chapel Mausoleum, Gate of Heaven Cemetery, East Hanover, New Jersey, as well as the Mausoleum of the Good Shepherd, St. Gertrude's Cemetery, Colonia, New Jersey (figure 56). For the Church of St. Elizabeth Ann Seton, Shrub Oak, New York, he worked with Rohlf's Stained and Leaded Glass Studios, Mount Vernon, New York using sandblasted and painted techniques.

BIBLIOGRAPHY Richard Goss, "As Told by the Artists: A Look at the Work of Albinas Elskus," *Stained Glass* 96/1 (Spring 2001), 40–47, and Sarah Brown, "Albinas Elskus, an American Master," *The Journal of Stained Glass* 20/1 (1996), 57–67.

FIGURE 57
Robert Pinart
Fabricated by Wilmark Studio
Resurrection Cross, **1987**
St. Luke's Episcopal Church, Long Beach, CA

ROBERT PINART (1927–) was born in Paris and graduated from the École Nationale Supérieure des Arts Décoratifs. At an early age he helped restore medieval church windows that had been dismantled in order to protect them from damage during World War II. He also worked in a number of studios making new work in Paris, including learning the *dalle-de-verre* technique in the studio of Auguste Labouret, with whom he produced the *Beatitudes* windows for St. Anne de Beaupre, Quebec, in 1948–49. In 1952 he came to the United States where he has collaborated as a designer for a number of studios including the Wilmark Studio, Pearl River, New York, and the Rambusch Decorating Company. His work may be found at the Bronx Zoo; Christ the King Lutheran Church, Cloudland, Oregon; and the National Cathedral, Washington, D.C. The depth of Pinart's symbolic skill as well as his great facility in design and draftsmanship appear in St. Luke's Episcopal Church, Long Beach, California (figure 57). In Pinart's characteristic explosive composition, a red-drenched empty cloth swirls around a silver stain yellow cross. The red garments – triumphant body of Christ? – the fire of the Holy Spirit? – cloak a cross whose dead wood has already sprouted into a life-giving vine. Pinart continues to create, such as the eleven windows for the Temple Sholom, Greenwich, Connecticut, installed in the main sanctuary in 1995.

BIBLIOGRAPHY Richard L. Hoover, "Robert Pinart: An Interview," *Stained Glass* 85 (Summer 1990), 98–105, 140–41.

FIGURE 58
Sylvia Nicolas
St. John the Evangelist,
1990s
Collection of the artist

SYLVIA NICOLAS (1928–) was born in the Netherlands and has produced a wide range of work including mosaics and sculpture as well as traditional leaded glass. Recent work includes the sixty-one stained glass panels for the new St. Dominic Chapel for Providence College, Providence, Rhode Island. She comes from a long tradition of stained glass artists. Her great grandfather Frans Nicolas (1926–1894) began a studio in Roermond, Netherlands in 1855. His son continued in the tradition, expanding the business by adding a studio in New York City. Nicolas's father Joep (1897–1971) exerted enormous influence on stained glass in Europe with the design of the St. Martin window for the *Exposition Internationale des Arts Décoratifs et Industriels Modernes* in Paris of 1925. In 1939, the impending war caused Joep to move his family to New York City. In the United States he did freelance work for the Rambusch Decorating Company and intermingled with progressive young artists. In 1954 Sylvia began a thirteen-year apprenticeship with her father, who in 1959 returned to Holland. *St. John the Evangelist* (figure 58) on display in the exhibition demonstrates the essential quality of Sylvia's painting style, reflecting a family tradition. The draftsmanship is fluid and open and the central figure blends into the background.

BIBLIOGRAPHY Diego Semprum Nicolas, "The Fifth Generation," *Stained Glass* 94 (Spring 1999), 41–46, 59 and Sylvia Nicolas, "The Saga Continues," Ibid., 59–61.

FIGURE 59

Jean-Jacques Duval

Fabricated by Rohlf's Stained & Leaded Glass Studio

Hebrew Tabernacle (interior), 1988

Washington Heights, NY, NY

JEAN-JACQUES DUVAL (1930–) has been a prolific designer for American studios. Born in Strasbourg, France he studied at the École des Arts Décoratifs, Strasbourg and at the Art Student's League, New York. He has designed stained glass, sculpture, and tapestries and mosaics with Rohlf's Stained and Leaded Glass Studios in Mount Vernon, New York. Like Robert Pinart he has produced in both the *dalle-de-verre*, exemplified by the windows for the Westville Synagogue, New Haven, Connecticut and in the traditional leaded technique exemplified by the windows of the Hebrew Tabernacle of Washington Heights installed in 1988 (figure 59). The rectilinear format of the architecture at Hebrew Tabernacle is reflected in the design of the window – the pattern, excluded to a frame shape, clearly incorporates the dedication of the window.

FIGURE 60
Saara Gallin
Mezuzah, **1999**
Collection of the artist

SAARA GALLIN (1930–) has worked in non-traditional stained glass and since the 1970s has appeared in juried shows at the Glassmasters Guild, The Corning Museum of Glass, and The Society for Arts and Crafts, Boston, Massachusetts, as well as solo shows in New York galleries and at Sarah Lawrence College, in Bronxville. She has also curated exhibitions on stained glass, including *Personal Vision/Silent Voices* for the New York Experimental Glass Workshop. Gallin's work, like that of artists such as Stephen Knapp and Mark Eric Gulsrud, is often sculptural, reflecting a three-dimensional presence. She uses a wide variety of techniques including etched, laminated, and kiln-formed glass. She also continues traditional leaded or copper foil work, as in *Mezuzah* (figure 60) on display in the exhibition. A mezuzah is a ritual object that is a reminder of Jewish faith – biblical verses inscribed on parchment, rolled up, inserted in a case, and attached to all doorposts of the house. This is in fulfillment of the command, "And thou shalt write them (the words of God) in the entry and on the doors of thy house" Deuteronomy 6.9, repeated later in Deuteronomy 11.20. The text is the familiar exhortation to Israel "Hear, O Israel, the Lord our God is One" and following, taken from the same two passages in Deuteronomy, 6.4–9 and 11.13–21. Gallin mixes Hebrew and English inscriptions in a freestanding form that appears as a sentinel, proclaiming the threshold of spiritual reflection.

FIGURE 61

Charles Z. Lawrence

Chancel windows, 1980s

St. John's Episcopal Church, Southampton NY

CHARLES Z. LAWRENCE (1935–) began his prolific career with a four-year apprenticeship at the Rudolph H. Buenz Studio in Newton, New Jersey. In 1960 he moved to New York City where he studied at the Pratt Art Institute and worked as a studio designer, notably for the Rambusch Decorating Company, New York City, and also as an independent designer. He remembers the examples of Robert Pinart and Robert Sowers, then also working at Rambusch. Lawrence produced a wide variety of faceted and leaded glass commissions, among them five windows for the National Cathedral in Washington, D.C.: *Ministering Angels, The Reformation, Raising of Lazarus, Healing Arts*, and the *Bloomberg Memorial*. Remarkably adept in both traditional figural work and abstraction, Lawrence remarked that Ludwig Schaffrath's influence away from the image "changed the face of stained glass for the better." At St. John's Episcopal Church, Southampton, New York, installed in 1976, Lawrence's abstracted seascape bathes the altar in a green-blue light (figure 61).

BIBLIOGRAPHY Victoria M. Kearney, "Profile: Charles Ziegler Lawrence," *Stained Glass* 87 (Fall 1992), 179–82, 217; Helene Weiss, "The Evolution of a Stained Glass Artist: A Conversation with Charles Z. Lawrence," Ibid. (Spring 1987), 10–22, quote at 20; Norman Temme, "Charles Z. Lawrence. A Twenty Year Dream Come True," Ibid. 74 (Winter 1979–80), 289–93.

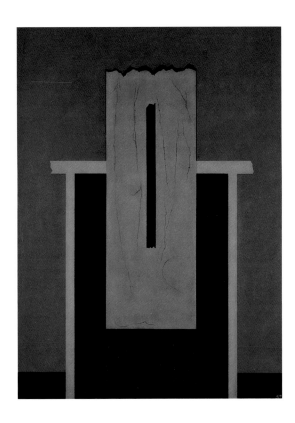

FIGURE 62
Robert Kehlmann
Entombment, Station 14, **1982**
The Corning Museum
of Glass, Corning, NY

ROBERT KEHLMANN (1942–), of Berkeley, California, speaks of his indebtedness to Robert Sowers's writings as well as to a broad range of American art. Kehlmann is explicit about his works not being windows, but autonomous objects. His *Entombment, Station 14,* of 1982 (figure 62), on display in the exhibition, uses layers of flat glass sandblasted on three surfaces to evoke an image of the tomb of Christ. The post-and-lintel background form recalls the opening of a rock-cut tomb while the overlay rectangle suggests a sarcophagus, but also the weightlessness of Christ's resurrected body in a hovering position on the picture plane. Kehlmann states: "By keeping my compositions subdued I try not to exploit people's instinctive attraction to colored light. My pieces are not 'colorful' in the Gothic and Tiffany stained glass window traditions that stress strong color contrasts. Rather, activity of brightness and color are subordinated to activity of form and line." Kehlmann also stresses the 'objectness' of each piece, with the ideal installation inviting the viewer to move around the work.

BIBLIOGRAPHY Robert Kehlmann, "Lead and Glass Drawings," *Stained Glass* 73 (Fall 1978), 180–82, quote on 181.

FIGURE 63

Ed Carpenter

Olson-Sundberg: architects

Fabricated by Douglas Hansen

Altar window and screen, 1997

St. Mark's Cathedral, Seattle, WA

ED CARPENTER (1946–), a prolific and admired designer in glass, received his education from the University of California at Santa Barbara and Berkeley. He later studied stained glass design and technique with Patrick Reyntiens in England, and large architectural glass design with Ludwig Schaffrath In Germany.[16] Located in Portland, Oregon, Carpenter has received numerous public and corporate commissions for his windows and sculptures, including the entrance area of the former Exxon Building at 1251 Avenue of the Americas at Rockefeller Center in New York City, and the Queens Civil Court. He has served on the Board of Trustees of the American Craft Enterprises, the American Craft Council, the Oregon School of Arts and Crafts, and the Hillside Center Artist's Cooperative. From 1985 to 1989, Carpenter served as the Metropolitan Arts Commissioner for Portland, Oregon where he also founded the Public Art Advisory Committee. In 1997, for St. Mark's Cathedral in Seattle, Washington (figure 63), Carpenter worked with Olson-Sundberg Architects to create a major window and reredos (screen) behind the altar. The glass fabrication using translucent, dichroic, and kiln-fused glass, was by Douglas Hansen, represented in this exhibition by windows for the Ignatius Chapel of Seattle University, Washington.

BIBLIOGRAPHY "New Glass Graces a Historic New York Skyscraper," *Stained Glass* 88 (Summer 1993), 128–29.

FIGURE 64
James Carpenter
Dichroic Light Field
(detail), 1995
New York, NY

JAMES CARPENTER (1949–) graduated from the Rhode Island School of Design, Providence, Rhode Island in 1972. He is the founder of James Carpenter Design Associates, New York, a collaborative studio dedicated to exploring new and emerging glass technologies. His commissions are international and include London, Berlin, and Genoa, as well as major cities in the United States such as New York, San Francisco and Portland. Many artists are strong voices in the contemporary field and exert a strong influence on all designers, even if the majority of their work is secular. Carpenter's work, like that of Stephen Knapp, is at the intersection of sculpture and architecture. Carpenter's *Dichroic Light Field* of 1995 (figure 64) is set at the intersection of Columbus Avenue and 68th Street, New York City. The changing light of the day strikes the fins of dichroic glass with different saturation and at different angles, creating constant shifts of color and density, acting as a foil to and reflection of the colors of the sky.

BIBLIOGRAPHY Andrew Moor, "Glass Sculpture: Jamie Carpenter," *Architectural Glass Art*, New York, 1997, 150–53.

MARK ERIC GULSRUD (1950–) earned a B.A. from California Lutheran University in 1972 and an M. F. A. from the University of Puget Sound, Seattle, in 1977. Additionally, he spent three summers at The Pilchuck Glass School in Stanwood, Washington, from 1977 to 1980. His work has shown consistent sensitivity to the translucency of material and the ability to combine abstract elements of architectural form and color with evocative imagery. He states of his commissions that "whether public, corporate, or liturgical, there exists the potential for the creation of a spiritual oasis; a space conducive to calm, healing, and personal growth." In the Resurrection Lutheran Church, Tuscon, Arizona, 1988 (figure 65), an ascending image of the resurrected Christ counterbalances a landscape of sweeping curves, revealing the actual landscape setting through clear and translucent sections of glass. The result is as if the spiritual reality of Christ's triumph becomes imprinted on the world he created. Like many other contemporary artists in glass, he has designed objects in cast and fused glass, liturgical furniture, and screens such as a 2002 laminated mouth-blown glass screen for the Sisters of St. Joseph in Orange, California.

BIBLIOGRAPHY John Seaton, "Windows of Clarity and Intent," *Stained Glass* 85 (Summer, 1990), 123–26.

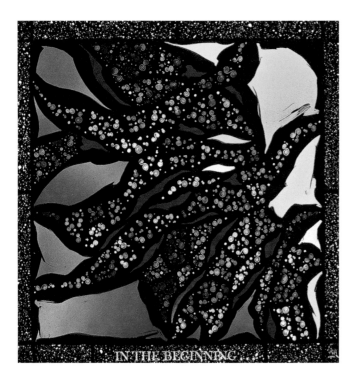

FIGURE 66
Mary Clerkin Higgins
In the Beginning, 2002
Collection of the artist

MARY CLERKIN HIGGINS (1954–) received her BA from Fordham University in 1976 and began an apprenticeship with the Greenland Studio in New York City that same year. In 1986, she opened her own studio, Clerkin Higgins Stained Glass, also located in New York City. Her work has relied heavily on painted glass, specifically vitreous paint and silver stain and her windows are notable for their inclusion of found as well as cast objects (figure 66). A highly respected stained glass conservator and restorer, she has worked on medieval and Renaissance glass in museum collections, most notably panels at the Metropolitan Museum of Art and its medieval collection at The Cloisters. She has also conserved glass by nineteenth and twentieth century artists, including Edward Burne-Jones, William Morris, Harry Clarke, John La Farge, Louis Comfort Tiffany, Frank Lloyd Wright, Marc Chagall, Henri Matisse, and Fernand Léger. Clerkin Higgins has worked with the artist, Rowan Le Compte, making two of his clerestory windows for the National Cathedral in Washington, D.C. and, most recently, selecting and painting a large window from his sketch for a church in New Bern, North Carolina. Her own commissions include two new windows in the Morgan Stanley/Lehman Brothers building in midtown Manhattan.

FIGURE 67
J. Kenneth Leap
**Fabricated by Derix Glasstudios,
Taunusstein, Germany**
Peaceable Kingdom, 2002
Collection of the artist

J. KENNETH LEAP (1964–) graduated in 1986 from the Glass Program of the Rhode Island School of Design, Providence, Rhode Island. His studio is a part of The Museum of American Glass, Wheaton Village, Millville, New Jersey. Like other artists interested in painting on glass, Leap has worked at the Pilchuck Glass School, Stanwood, Washington, as well as studied with Albinas Elskus in a glass workshop at the Parsons School of Design, New York City. In 1993, he executed the *Symbols of State Medallions* for the State House Annex in Trenton, New Jersey, to complement windows designed in 1929 by William Sotter. For the Masonic Home Chapel, Burlington, New Jersey he designed an altar window based on Isaiah 40.31: "They that wait upon the Lord shall renew their strength, they shall mount up with wings as eagles." The inspiration for the window in this exhibition is also taken from Isaiah 11.6–9, the often-cited ideal of the *Peaceable Kingdom* (figure 67) where the lamb and the lion "shall abide together and a little child shall lead them." The juxtaposition of his symbols calls to mind Henri Rousseau's "naive" paintings, while the meticulous realism is close to fifteenth-century Lowlands artists such as Jan van Eyck.

BIBLIOGRAPHY Helene Weis, "Kenneth Leap: Ecologist, Photographer and Stained Glass Artist" *Stained Glass* 90 (Fall 1995), 197–99, 229–31; Helene Weis, "A Natural View," ibid. 85 (Fall 1990), 202–5.

THE BREADTH OF GLASS ART CANNOT BE COVERED HERE.

INNOVATIVE ARTISTS CONTINUE TO PIONEER THE MEDIUM OF GLASS, ARTISTS SUCH AS **JUDITH SCHAECHTER** (1961–). SINCE GRADUATING FROM THE RHODE ISLAND SCHOOL OF DESIGN'S GLASS PROGRAM IN 1983, SHE HAS EXHIBITED WIDELY IN GALLERIES, INCLUDING THE 2002 WHITNEY BIENNIAL. HER VIGOROUS FIGURAL STYLE IN THE GERMAN EXPRESSIONIST TRADITION HAS EARNED HER INCLUSION IN THE PHILADELPHIA MUSEUM OF ART, THE CORNING MUSEUM OF GLASS, THE RENWICK GALLERY OF THE SMITHSONIAN INSTITUTION, AND THE METROPOLITAN MUSEUM OF ART, AMONG OTHERS. ARTISTS, LIKE **NARCISSUS QUAGLIATA** (1942–), HAVE ALSO ENTERED PRESTIGIOUS COLLECTIONS, SUCH AS THE VICTORIA AND ALBERT MUSEUM AND THE CORNING MUSEUM OF GLASS.[17] **PAUL MARIONI** (1941–) AND **PETER MOLLICA** (1941–) CONTINUE TO DEVELOP THE FIELD AND TEACH A NEW GENERATION OF ARTISTS.

ENDNOTES

1 Benoit Gilsoul, *Stained Glass* 80 (Fall 1985), 247.

2 John Piper, "Art or AntiArt," in: Brian Clarke, ed., *Architectural Stained Glass* (New York, 1979), 60.

3 Ludwig Schaffrath, "The Situation of Glass Painting in the U. S. A.," *New Work* (January 1982): 27; Konrad Pfaff, *Ludwig Schaffrath: Stained Glass and Mosaic* (Krefeld, 1977). The tradition of German progressive art in stained glass is long. The Bauhaus had a department of stained glass headed by Josef Albers (1881–1976), who later taught at the Yale University School of Art. See his sandblasted panel *Overlapping*, 1927, Busch-Reisinger Museum Harvard University; Friedericke Kitschen, "Josef Albers," in: Jeannine Fiedler/Peter Feierabend, *Bauhaus* (Cologne, 1999), 308–19.

4 Lutz Haufschild, "The Pilchuck Glass School: Teaching What Cannot be Taught," *Stained Glass* 78 (Spring 1983), 23–39.

5 The painting is a gift of Barbara W. McCue and Gerald M. McCue to the Museum of Fine Arts, Boston.

6 Walter Hopps/Dominique De Menil, *The Menil Collection: A Selection from the Paleolithic to the Modern Era* (New York 1997), 314–16.

7 Charles Pratt/Joan Pratt, "Gabriel Loire: A Contemporary French Master," *Stained Glass* 82 (Spring 1987): 31–36.

8 Andrew Moor, *Architectural Glass Art* (New York, 1997), 55.

9 Ibid., 58–59

10 Jack Coward/Sue Scott, *Proof Positive: Forty Years of Contemporary American Printmaking at ELAE, 1957–1997*, exh. cat., Corcoran Gallery of Art (Washington D.C., 1997).

11 Moor, *Architectural Glass Art*, 66–68.

12 See Robert Marteau, *The Stained Glass Windows of Chagall 1957–1970* (New York, 1973), profiling seven major commissions. For the Jerusalem windows see http://www.hadassah.org.il/chagall.htm

13 Janet McNally, "Chagall in Glass," *Stained Glass* 80 (Fall 1985), 227–31.

14 Robert Sowers, *The Lost Art* (London, 1954), 23–50.

15 Arthur Stern, "Three Award-Winning Collaborations," *Stained Glass* 93 (Spring 1998), 38–43. Other projects include the Italian Cemetery Mausoleum Chapel, Colma, CA, and Christ Church Episcopal, Portola Valley, CA, also honored by IFRAA, The Interfaith Forum on Religion, Art and Architecture, an affiliate of The American Institute of Architects. *The Stations of the Cross* received IFRAA's Award for Art in Religious Buildings in 1990.

16 See Peter Mollica, "Schaffrath at Burleighfield House," *Stained Glass* 70 (Fall & Winter 1975), 113–16. Burleighfield House, Loudwater, halfway between London and Oxford

17 Moor, *Architectural Glass Art*, 136–39.

STAINED GLASS WINDOW FABRICATION
BY PATRICIA C. PONGRACZ

… I saw the sanctuary filled with a variety of all kinds of differing colors, displaying the utility and nature of each pigment. I entered it unseen and immediately filled the storeroom of my heart fully with all these things. I examined them one by one with careful experiment testing them all by eye and by hand, and I have committed them to you in clarity and without envy for your study. Since this method of painting [on glass] cannot be obvious, I worked hard like a careful investigator using every means to learn by what skilled arts the variety of pigments could decorate the work without repelling the daylight and the rays of the sun.

Theophilus, *On Divers Arts*, prologue to Book II, 12th century[1]

The making of a stained glass window, whether for a church, synagogue, mausoleum, office, hospital or home, is and has always been a multi-step process involving various people. A glassmaker produces glass, a distributor sells it, an artist designs the window that a glass studio or fabricator makes. Tracing window fabrication from the production of glass beginning in the pot to its final form in a window allows us to appreciate the complexity of this architectural art. The following essay, by no means exhaustive, is an introduction to the history of glass-making and to the varied techniques employed by artists working today, six of whom are profiled in Chapter 7. Brief descriptions of many of the firms involved in the current production of stained glass in the United States may be found at the end of this chapter.

I. MAKING GLASS

THEN TAKE TWO PARTS OF ASHES... AND A THIRD PART OF SAND, COLLECTED OUT OF WATER, AND CAREFULLY CLEANED OF EARTH AND STONES. MIX THEM IN A CLEAN PLACE, AND WHEN THEY HAVE BEEN LONG AND WELL MIXED TOGETHER LIFT THEM UP WITH THE LONG-HANDLED IRON LADLE AND PUT THEM ON THE UPPER HEARTH IN THE SMALLER SECTION OF THE FURNACE SO THAT THEY MAY BE FRITTED.

Theophilus, *On Divers Arts,* Book II, Chapter 4, 12th century[2]

Evidence of written recipes for making glass date as far back as the second millennium BC where it was recorded in cuneiform impressed on clay tablets.[3] Though technological advances have allowed glass to be used in new ways over the course of the twentieth century, the core processes for mixing, painting and firing stained glass follow the precepts recorded by various writers over time since antiquity. Sand (silica), lime, and potash or soda (alkali), are the raw or batch materials used to make the glass melt. Mixed together in ceramic pots and heated in a furnace to at least 2200 degrees Fahrenheit, the batch materials undergo chemical changes, turning into a molten liquid that when cooled becomes the hard, brittle material we know as glass.[4]

Chemistry

THERE IS A STORY THAT ONCE A SHIP BELONGING TO SOME TRADERS IN NATURAL SODA [NITRUM] PUT IN [AT PTOLEMAIS] AND THAT THEY SCATTERED ALONG THE SHORE TO PREPARE A MEAL. SINCE, HOWEVER, NO STONES SUITABLE FOR SUPPORTING THEIR CAULDRONS WERE FORTHCOMING, THEY RESTED THEM ON LUMPS OF SODA FROM THEIR CARGO. WHEN THESE BECAME HEATED AND WERE COMPLETELY MINGLED WITH THE SAND ON THE BEACH A STRANGE TRANSLUCENT LIQUID FLOWED FORTH IN STREAMS; AND THIS, IT IS SAID, WAS THE ORIGIN OF GLASS.

Pliny the Elder, *Natural History,* Book 36, 191, 1st century AD[5]

Pliny's anecdote, although usually regarded as apocryphal, is repeated throughout the literature on glassmaking since the early Middle Ages. It is an apt introduction to the basic chemistry of glassmaking.[6] Glass, like metal or fabric, is a word used to describe a broad category of like material.[7] Within the category glass are numerous glasses, each with its own chemical composition that determines specific properties, like softening point and durability. Analyzing the chemical components of glasses yields insight to its time, place and method of production.[8] For example, certain batch materials may be found in specific geographic regions or may have been widely used at a particular time in a particular place. For these reasons, the chemistry, briefly outlined below, is as interesting and artful a consideration as the production methods discussed later in this essay.

Though its production has changed over time ensuring more predictable results, the glass made for stained glass windows still follows the basic principles outlined in the earliest glassmaking texts.[9] In scientific terms, glasses need three components: a network former, a flux, and a stabilizer.[10] The network is the glasses' chemical skeleton composed of oxygen (O) and silicon (Si) that form silicate chains. A glass network is best visualized as an irregular chainlink-like structure (figure 68). Sand or in some cases finely ground pebbles are the raw materials for introducing silica.

A flux is added to the silica to reduce its melting point, allowing the batch materials to change state at a lower temperature. In soda-silica glasses, sodium carbonate (Na_2CO_3) or soda is the flux. The sodium ions, illustrated by the autonomous line-filled circles, are scattered throughout the silicate network. The majority of glasses made in the Middle East from around 1500 BC until the thirteenth century were soda-lime-silica glasses.[11] The source of the raw material for soda was usually natron, abundant in Egypt in natural deposits around certain lakes.[12] Natron lowers the melting point of silica allowing it to change into liquid state, aptly noted by the shipwrecked sailors cooking their dinner on the sands of Ptolemais described in Pliny's anecdote.

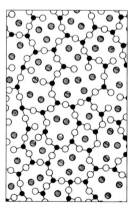

FIGURE 68
Soda Silica Glass

Schematic drawing, Glass network

R. H. Brill

FIGURE 69
Opalescent glass

Kokomo Opalescent Glass, Kokomo, IN

In Europe in the Middle Ages, the majority of glasses made were potash-lime-silica glasses ($K_2O:CaO:SiO_2$), although soda-lime-silica ($Na_2O:CaO:SiO_2$) and mixed alkalai glasses (($Na_2O + K_2O):CaO:SiO_2$)), where soda and potash are present in equal concentrations, were also sometimes produced.[13] Eraclius writing in *De Coloribus et Artibus Romanorum* in fact instructed that glass "is made with the ashes of both fern and of 'fania' – that is the small trees which grow in the woods."[14] The use of plant ash or potash (K_2O) as flux makes sense when one considers the readily obtainable supplies of ferns, trees, and even kelp or seaweed, all sources of plant ashes in Europe.[15]

Lime (CaO) is added to both potash-silica and soda-silica glasses as a stabilizer. Like the sodium ions, calcium ions are scattered throughout the silicate network. Its addition results in a glass that is less vulnerable to water corrosion. Lime must be added with care however, because too much actually reduces the stability of the glass.[16]

Though the chemistry of modern glassmaking has been considerably refined, most glass is still made from the basic batch materials of silica, lime and soda or potash.

Coloring glass

FOR STAINING [GLASS] SAPPHIRE, SILVER AND SULPHUR SHOULD BE SET ON THE FIRE TOGETHER; AFTERWARDS FROM 2 POUNDS OF CLEAR MOSAIC GLASS AND 3 OZ. OF THE ABOVE-MENTIONED SAPPHIRE COOKED TOGETHER, YOU WILL MAKE JACINTH STONES.
Mappae Clavicula, chapter 256, 12th century[17]

IF YOU WISH IT TO BECOME RED, YOU WILL DO AS FOLLOWS, WITH ASHES NOT WELL BAKED. TAKE COPPER FILINGS, BURN THEM UNTIL THEY ARE REDUCED TO POWDER, AND THEN THROW THEM INTO YOUR MELTING POTS; AND THIS WILL MAKE RED GLASS...
Eraclius, *De Coloribus et Artibus Romanorum,* Book III, chapter, VII, 12th century[18]

Stained or colored glass is produced by mixing metal oxides into the glass melt. For example, the addition of manganese makes purple glass; iron, green glass; cobalt, blue glass. The concentration and composition of the oxide determines the saturation or depth of the glass's color.[19] The addition of the colorant results in a sheet of glass that is colored throughout. Such glass is often known as pot metal glass because it is made in the pot.

Flashed glass for stained glass windows, where a thin layer of colored glass coats the surface of clear glass, was employed in the Middle Ages to make red glass. It is produced while the glass is still hot by coating a clear glass gather with colored glass and then blowing it. Opalescent glass, widely used at the turn of the twentieth century by designers like Tiffany and La Farge, is a milky, opaque glass made by mixing various colors of molten glass together (figure 69). These processes are discussed below.

The texture of glass

Straw marks, bubbles, ripples, folds, and assorted other features and textures add to the depth of the palette used by the contemporary glass artist. Bubbles (known as seeds, if they are very small) occur in the mixing of the glass. These tiny pockets of trapped air are today considered the mark of authentic, mouth blown antique glass and are a desirable component of art glass. The formation of seeds is often encouraged by dropping a sodden piece of wood or even a potato into the molten glass to release gas into the mix to produce the bubbles.[20] The texture of glass is often the result of its method of manufacture. Glass can be blown, rolled and molded, processes that are described below.

FIGURE 70

Blowing Glass

Glashütte Lamberts,
Waldsassen, Germany

FIGURE 71

Opening glass balloon

Glashütte Lamberts,
Waldsassen, Germany

FIGURE 72

Flattening sheet

Glashütte Lamberts,
Waldsassen, Germany

FIGURE 73

Making glass roundel

Glashütte Lamberts,
Waldsassen, Germany

FIGURE 74

Finishing roundel

Glashütte Lamberts,
Waldsassen, Germany

Making Glass Sheets

AFTER BEING REDUCED TO LUMPS, THE GLASS IS AGAIN FUSED IN THE WORKSHOP AND IS TINTED. SOME OF IT IS SHAPED BY BLOWING, SOME MACHINED ON A LATHE AND SOME CHASED LIKE SILVER.
Pliny, *Natural History,* Book 36, 193,
first century AD[21]

Blown Glass

Though a sheet of glass can now be made in a variety of ways, the traditional muff or cylinder and crown methods are still used today.[22] In the former, the glassmaker swirls a ball of molten glass, called a gather, onto the end of a blowpipe. Turning the pipe, a glassmaker blows the malleable ball into a long, narrow balloon of glass. As the balloon of glass lengthens, the glassmaker lays it in a wooden trough to support it while it is being turned (figure 70). The trough's surface leaves long, thin, straw-like marks in the glass. Once the balloon has reached the desired size, the bottom is snipped off, opened and smoothed (figure 71). The top is separated from the pipe and opened turning the balloon into a cylinder. Once the cylinder has cooled, it is scored on one side and put into a furnace with its scored side up. When the glass again becomes softened, the cylinder is coaxed open with the aid of a rod until it flattens and can be smoothed into a sheet (figure 72). Today, glass made using this method is known as antique glass. Glashütte Lamberts, Waldsassen, Germany is a major producer of antique glass.

In the crown method of glassmaking, the glassmaker blows the gather into a balloon as in the muff or cylinder method described above. Once the balloon reaches the desired size it is snipped open, transferred to a second pipe called a pontil and spun. The centrifugal force opens the now cut balloon into a round plate-like piece of class called a crown. Once the diameter of the crown has

reached the desired size, it is cracked off the pontil and left to cool. The center of the sheet is thicker and retains a scar where the pontil was attached. Called a bull's-eye, it was often used in windows as a decorative embellishment beginning in the Middle Ages. Rarely, the thick, uneven bull's-eye was cut and leaded into a window like a normal piece of glass.[23] Today, glass roundels are made following the crown method (figure 73, 74). Roundels, which mimic the characteristics of bull's-eyes, are still used as decorative embellishments.

Cooling

WHEN THE GLASS IS COMPLETELY FLAT, IMMEDIATELY TAKE IT OUT AND PUT IT IN THE ANNEALING FURNACE, WHICH SHOULD BE MODERATELY HOT, IN SUCH A WAY THAT THE SHEET DOES NOT LIE DOWN BUT STANDS UP AGAINST THE WALL. NEXT TO IT PUT ANOTHER SHEET, FLATTENED OUT IN THE SAME WAY, AND A THIRD, AND ALL THE REST.
Theophilus, *On Divers Arts,* Book II, Chapter 9,
12th century[24]

Glass, regardless of its manufacture, must be cooled slowly to minimize internal strains. If left to cool on its own at room temperature, glass cools unevenly: the exterior cools into a solidified state before the interior. Once the exterior has solidified it cannot "give" to allow for changes on the interior as it cools. This results in internal strain inherent in the glass that weakens it. Cooling the glass at a controlled temperature over time in an annealing furnace allows all of the material to set up at the same rate and results in a stronger, relatively strain free glass.[25]

FIGURE 75
"Torn flash" glass
Glashütte Lamberts,
Waldsassen, Germany

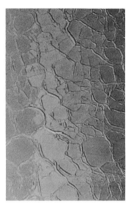

FIGURE 76
Crackled glass
Glashütte Lamberts,
Waldsassen, Germany

FIGURE 77
Reamy glass
Glashütte Lamberts,
Waldsassen, Germany

Different Blown Glasses

As mentioned above, flashed glass has been used in stained glass windows since the Middle Ages. Today, flashed glass is made in various colors and densities. To make it, a gather of the flash color is blown into a balloon. Its shape determines the color saturation of the final sheet. For example, a round balloon will make an evenly colored sheet; a pear-shaped balloon an unevenly shaded sheet; and a balloon that has been "notched" produces a sheet of swirled variegated colors (figure 75).[26] The balloon is dipped into the base color glass, often clear, and the now-combined balloon is blown into a cylinder from which the sheet of flashed glass is made.

Crackled and reamy glasses are notable for their textures inherent in their matrices. Both mouth blown, their characteristic textures result from specific modifications made during the blowing process. Crackled glass (figure 76) has a scaly surface texture similar to a reptile's skin that is produced when the hot glass balloon is momentarily dipped in cold water. Small surface breaks occur when the temperature changes quickly from hot to cold. After it is

pulled from the water the balloon is reheated to heal the breaks and then blown into a cylinder from which the scaly textured sheet is made.

Reamy glass is characterized by the marked swirls and large bubbles known as "ox-eyes" (figure 77). The swirls, which resemble rippling water, are made when glass shards are added to the molten glass. The shards in the gather impress the glass balloon as it is blown producing the swirling rivulets. The reamy glass balloon is blown into a cylinder from which the sheet is made.

Rolled Glass

Rolled glass can be hand or machine made. In the latter, ladles full of molten glass are scooped out of the ceramic pot in the furnace and carried to the mixing table (figure 78).[27] To ensure that the glass cools evenly, the people carrying the ladles must rock them as they transfer the glass from the furnace to the mixing table (figure 79). Once on the table the glass is mixed and smoothed by the tableperson and then fed into rollers like paper through a printing press (figure 80). Texture is added to the surface of the sheet by a

FIGURE 78

Taking molten glass from the furnace

Kokomo Opalescent
Glass, Kokomo, IN

FIGURE 79

Carrying the ladle

Kokomo Opalescent
Glass, Kokomo, IN

FIGURE 80

Ladling the glass onto the table

Kokomo Opalescent
Glass, Kokomo, IN

FIGURE 81

Rolling the glass

Kokomo Opalescent
Glass, Kokomo, IN

patterned roller (figure 81). Kokomo Opalescent glass in Kokomo, Indiana is one of the oldest manufactures of opalescent glass in the United States.[28]

Hand Rolled Glass

Like its machine-made counterpart, hand-rolled glass is ladled onto a steel tabletop while still molten, approximately 1900 degrees Fahrenheit.[29] To make opalescent glass, different colors are ladled onto the tabletop and then mixed by hand using long steel rods. The molten glass, called a gob, is then manually forced through moving rollers using steel rods. The glass may have a texture on one side depending on the type of rollers used (figures 82, 83, 84).

Uroboros specializes in making hand made opalescent glass in the manner of the glass used by Louis Comfort Tiffany and is known for its line of Tiffany style drapery, steamer/fracture and ring mottle glass. Drapery glass is made by ladling the molten glass onto the steel tabletop and then rolling the glass by hand with a large steel pipe similar to the way dough is rolled with a rolling pin. The glass-maker manipulates the malleable glass into ripples that mimic the fall of drapery (figure 85). Drapery glass was used by Tiffany to suggest the billows and fall of a figure's clothing (see figures 15, 17).

Fracture/streamer glass is characterized by the thin lines and small shards of glass embedded in the glass's surface (figure 86). To make the glass chips or fractures, the desired color is blown into a large balloon of thin glass. Once cool, it is broken into shards that are then placed on the steel tabletop. Thin lines of glass, the streamers, are then drizzled like icing among the fractures. Ladles full of molten glass are then poured on top of the fractures and streamers and the glass is hand rolled in the method described above. Tiffany often used streamer/fracture or confetti glass to suggest foliage.

Ring Mottle glass is very similar in appearance to mold growth. The organic looking nature of the glass is the result of forced crystalline growth

FIGURE 82
Fibroid textured glass
Uroboros Glass Studios, Portland, OR

FIGURE 83
Herringbone granite ripple
Uroboros Glass Studios, Portland, OR

FIGURE 84
Iridescent granite ripple
Uroboros Glass Studios, Portland, OR

FIGURE 85
Drapery glass
Uroboros Glass Studios, Portland, OR

FIGURE 86
Fracture/streamer glass
Uroboros Glass Studios, Portland, OR

in the matrices of two different glasses. The competing crystalline structures result in the subtle color shadings characteristic of the "rings" (figure 87). Like the fracture/streamer glass, ring mottle is often used to suggest foliage.

Molded or Kiln-formed Glass

Molded or kiln-formed glass is made by firing solid glass pieces, in the form of sheets, billets or frit, into a mold. A plaster mold can be made or a design can be pressed into casting sand. Once the mold is ready, glass is placed into it and heated slowly in a kiln. When the glass becomes softened it conforms to the shape of the mold (figure 88; see also figure 98). Like sheet glass, the kiln-formed glass relief must anneal. Architectural kiln-formed glass is then tempered in a kiln to strengthen it.

Fused Glass

Fused glass refers to sheets of glass with similar properties that are made to be heated together in a kiln until they melt together. As mentioned above, different glasses have different properties depending upon their chemical compositions. Not all glasses are compatible: melting points differ as do annealing rates and tensile strengths. Fused glasses are compatible; they expand and contract at the same rate, meaning that they will melt at the same temperature and cool at the same rate insuring that they can fuse without breaking. They are made to be arranged together into designs or decorative compositions (figure 95).

Float Glass

Introduced in the 1950s by Sir Alastair Pilkington, float glass is the ordinary, mass produced glass most often found in window panes. It is used as the base or substrate for fusing, casting or kiln-forming glass and it is often the glass of choice for sandblasting, acid etching and enamelling (figures 90, 92–94). The mechanically-made, clear, flawless, flat glass is produced by floating together molten glass and molten tin. The glass is poured from the furnace in an uninterrupted stream into the tin bath. The tin and glass repel one another, much like oil and water. The suspension of glass above tin results in a smooth glass surface. From the bath the float glass is cooled in an annealing furnace, and then cut.

Dichroic Glass

For contemporary glass artists dichroic glass refers to a particular type of coated glass characterized by its reflective, iridescent quality (figures 64, 111, 112). It is produced by firing thin layers of metallic oxides onto the glass using the Vapor Deposition method:

The deposition occurs in a high vacuum chamber. The glass is suspended in the top of the chamber and rotated. The coating materials, titanium oxides, zirconium oxides, silicon oxides and aluminum oxides, are placed in crucibles at the bottom and bombarded with a high powered electron beam which is focused over the materials with electromagnetic fields. The heat generated by the beam, ranging from 1500 to 3000 degrees Celsius depending on the oxide, vaporizes the materials and the vapor condenses on the glass substrate.[30]

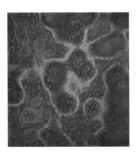

FIGURE 87
Ring mottle glass
Uroboros Glass Studios,
Portland, OR

FIGURE 88
**Molded or kiln-formed
float glass**
Derix Glasstudios,
Taunusstein, Germany

II. PAINTING ON GLASS

IN THE PROCESS OF WORKING WITH VITREOUS PAINTS OR ETCHING ACIDS, AS WELL AS SILVER STAINS AND THE FIRING OF PAINTED GLASS, ARTISTS COME INTO VERY CLOSE CONTACT WITH THE MYSTERIES OF THEIR MATERIALS. THE PHYSICAL CHANGES THAT ONE BRINGS TO THE SURFACE OF THE GLASS ARE THE RESULTS NOT ONLY OF HIS OR HER OWN EFFORTS, BUT ALSO THE MARKS OF INDIVIDUAL TALENT AND TECHNICAL SKILL. THIS CLOSE ENGAGEMENT PRODUCES A FEELING OF CONFIDENCE IN ONE'S ABILITY TO CONTROL LIGHT, COLOR, AND BALANCE IN WINDOWS OR PANELS.

Albinas Elskus, *The Art of Painting on Glass*, 1980[31]

Glass can be painted in a variety of ways. Paint may be applied manually using a brush or it may be sprayed using an airbrush, in freehand or through a stencil or silkscreen (figure 89). Glass paint is fired onto the glass so that it forms a permanent bond. Paint may be used to illustrate or highlight features described by the glass and lead or, in the case of enamels, it can be painted on glass like oil paint on a canvas.

Enamel

THEN WASH THE POWDER AND APPLY IT UPON YOUR GLASS AS YOU PLEASE AND LET THE COLOUR DRY THOROUGHLY; THEN PUT THE GLASS UPON THE RIM OF THE CHAMBER IN WHICH GLASSES ARE COOLED, ON THE SIDE FROM WHICH THE GLASSES ARE TAKEN OUT COLD, AND GRADUALLY INTRODUCE IT INTO THE CHAMBER TOWARDS THE FIRE WHICH COMES OUT OF THE FURNACE, AND TAKE CARE YOU DO NOT PUSH TOO FAST LEST THE HEAT SHOULD SPLIT IT, AND WHEN YOU SEE THAT IT IS THOROUGHLY HEATED, TAKE IT UP WITH THE "PONTELLO" AND FIX IT TO THE "PONTELLO" AND PUT IT IN THE MOUTH OF THE FURNACE HEATING IT AND INTRODUCING IT GRADUALLY. WHEN YOU SEE THAT THE SMALTI SHINE AND THAT THEY HAVE FLOWED WELL, TAKE THE GLASS

FIGURE 89
Silkscreen design on float glass
Derix Glasstudios, Taunusstein, Germany

FIGURE 90
David Fraser (1955–)/Indre Bileris (1973–)
***Prophet*, Display of painting techniques, 1990s**
St. Ann Center for Restoration and the Arts, New York, NY

FIGURE 91
Silverstain on float glass
Derix Glasstudios, Taunusstein, Germany

OUT AND PUT IT IN THE CHAMBER TO COOL, AND IT IS DONE.

Segreti per Colori, Chapter 7, #270, 15th century[32]

Enamel paint is a fine glass powder available in many colors. Like colored glasses, enamel paint derives its color from metal oxides. To paint with enamels the powder is mixed with an oily binder. The viscosity of the mixture depends on the manner in which the enamel will be applied: by paint brush, airbrush, freehand or stencil. When heated in the kiln, the binder evaporates; the powdered enamel becomes liquid and fuses to its glass substrate. Once cool, the enamel paint has a smooth, shiny surface (figures 101, 106).[33]

Neutral Trace Paint

Often details in stained glass windows, be they hands, faces, drapery fold lines, highlights or shadows, are painted and fired onto the glass. Vitreous paint is applied to the cut pieces of glass and then fired in the furnace until it adheres to the glass. Highlights may also be suggested using silver stain, a silver containing solution that turns

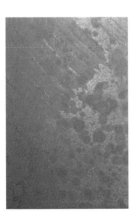

FIGURE 92
Acid etched float glass

Derix Glasstudios,
Taunusstein, Germany

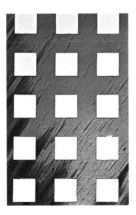

FIGURE 93
Sandblasted and enamelled float glass

Derix Glasstudios,
Taunusstein, Germany

yellow when fired (figure 91). It has been used to decorate glass for the past thousand years.[34]

III. DRAWING INTO GLASS

TO MAKE WATER FOR CUTTING GLASS.— TAKE VITRIOL, WHICH COMES UPON THE WALLS, AND MAKE A DISTILLED WATER FROM IT, AND KEEP IT IN A VESSEL WELL CLOSED. THEN TAKE ROMAN VITRIOL AND POUND IT WELL, DISTILL IT, AND KEEP THE WATER ALSO IN A CLOSE VESSEL; THEN TAKE SAL-AMMONIAC AND DISTILL IT, AND KEEP THIS ALSO. WHEN YOU WANT TO USE THE LIQUOR, TAKE EQUAL QUANTITIES OF EACH OF THESE WATERS, MIX THEM TOGETHER, AND DRAW WITH THE MIXED LIQUOR UPON THE GLASS, AND IT WILL BE CUT EXACTLY AS YOU LIKE WHEREVER IT IS WETTED WITH THIS WATER.

Segreti per Colori, 7th chapter, verse 217, 15th century[35]

In addition to adding texture during manufacture, etching and sandblasting are used to make designs on glass. The processes described below abrade or cut away at the surface of the glass and in many instances can be applied using painting techniques like stencils (figure 93).

Acid Etching is used to draw a design into glass by means of chemical corrosion (figure 92). The glass's surface is covered in a protective coating, called a resist, that can be made of wax, contact paper, anything that covers the surface preventing the acid from leaching through to the glass. Once the resist is applied, the design is cut or scratched through it to reveal the glass's surface. Hydrofluoric acid is then applied. The acid bites the glass, etching the surface in the desired design. The depth of the bite depends on the length of time the glass is exposed to the hydrofluoric acid.

Unlike acid etching, sandblasting abrades the glass's surface mechanically (figure 93). A resist, usually of dried wood glue or heavy contact paper, is applied to the glass and cut into the desired design. The glass is then put into an industrial sandblaster, a sealed chamber into which grit and air under high pressure are forced. The sandblaster has holes through which heavy gloves are inserted allowing the artist to reach in to handle the glass and direct the grit and air by means of a small hose with a nozzle. Like the spray of water through a garden hose, the nozzle's opening can be adjusted to define the flow of grit and the pressure with which it is applied. The artist uses the hose almost like a paint brush directing a steady stream of abrasive current onto the glass, applying design by means of abrasion.

III. MAKING A WINDOW

HE WILL COME TO YOU WITH THE MEASUREMENTS OF HIS WINDOW, THE WIDTH AND LENGTH: YOU WILL TAKE AS MANY SHEETS OF PAPER GLUED TOGETHER AS YOU NEED FOR YOUR WINDOW; AND YOU WILL DRAW YOUR FIGURE FIRST WITH CHARCOAL, THEN FIX IT WITH INK, WITH YOUR FIGURE COMPLETELY SHADED, EXACTLY AS YOU DRAW ON PANEL. THEN YOUR GLASS MASTER TAKES THIS DRAWING, AND SPREADS IT OUT ON A LARGE FLAT BENCH OR TABLE; AND PROCEEDS TO CUT HIS GLASSES, A SECTION AT A TIME, ACCORDING TO THE WAY HE WANTS TO THE COSTUMES OF THE FIGURE PAINTED.
Cennino Cennini, *Il libro dell'arte,* Section XI, 15th century[36]

As many of the artists in the following chapter articulate, making a stained glass window is a process of negotiation. To glaze a space one must consider architectural issues of light, volume, and size as well as the desires of the patron commissioning the window and the needs of the viewers seeing it over time. As the above quotation suggests, making a window has always involved a number of specially trained people: glassmakers to make the glass, artists to design the window, and fabricators to cut the glass and leads and assemble them into composition. Though each artist may have a different method of working the steps enumerated below outline the basic process for window fabrication.

The concept for a window design is first articulated in numerous sketches, drawings and small scale designs. In them, the artist works out how the window will look, chooses the colors, and the design elements. Over time these "pre-drawings" are worked into a formal, small-scale design for the window that is presented to the patron. Called a *vidimus* in the Middle Ages, today the model can either be drawn or generated on a computer.

From the model, the artist designs a full-size drawing for the window called a cartoon. This one-to-one scale drawing captures the detail of the window and becomes the pattern for it. Lead lines are drawn in heavy black line and a color key, identifying the color of each piece of glass, is included.

After the cartoon is drawn, the artist chooses the glass. Glass may be selected and bought directly from the manufacturer or through a distributor. Artists may consult a sample box of glass containing hundreds of various glass pieces each measuring approximately 2 x 2 inches. The manufacturer supplies the sample box to illustrate the breadth of glass produced. Examples of glass samples are pictured here (figures 82–87) and sample boxes from Uroboros, Kokomo Opalescent Glass and Glashütte Lamberts are on display in the exhibition.

An artist may choose glass from full size sheets either on site at the glass manufacturer or at a distributor like Bendheim, in Passaic, New Jersey, founded in 1927. Bendheim, the exclusive distributor for Glashütte Lamberts, has thousands of glass sheets in stock including glass produced by

Uroboros, Kokomo, Bullseye, and many others.

The selection process can take quite a long time because of the number of glasses produced today. The artist is interested in the glass's color, density (meaning how deeply saturated the color is), and texture. All affect how the light passes through the window once installed. Speaking about the importance of color in a stained glass window and its reception, Patrick Reyntiens wrote:

In glass the interval-structure, or how the colours are placed in relation to one another, between the stimuli of red or blue or white spread over the window is what gives the whole composition its vitality. How the eye takes in one stimulus followed by another – and the time-interval between the stimuli – is in many ways parallel to how the ear perceives the intervals in music.[37]

In Ellen Miret's windows for the Mausoleum Chapel, in Monsey, New York the glass is entirely unpainted; glass and leadlines alone create the images. She took care to choose textured glass for the clouds to suggest their billowy nature in the *Ascension* window (figure 108).

Once selected the glass is cut according to paper templates made from the cartoon. The cartoon is traced onto separate paper and cut into the shapes the glass will eventually take. The templates are lain upon the glass sheet and the glass is scored with a diamond cutter and snapped to the exact size. Edges are nibbled to their finished shape with a grozing pliers. Once cut, the glass is painted, enamelled, etched or sandblasted.

Each glass piece is fitted into an h-shaped strip of lead called a came which is nailed in place. Lead is pliable and can be bent to fit the curve of the glass. Once secured, the leads holding the glass pieces are soldered together and waterproofed.

Window glass may also be joined together by a process known as the copper foil technique where the edges of the glass are wrapped in copper foil and soldered. This reduces the graphic emphasis of the "leadlines," now relegated to the interstices between the glass. An example of copper foil technique is the O'Shaughnessy panel, *For the Glory of God*, (figure 25).

Plating glass sheets was often used by the Tiffany Studios in opalescent windows. To produce a desired color or texture effect multiple sheets of glass were stacked one upon the other and leaded together. This added depth and emphasis to a particular part of the composition (see figure 17).

In the *dalle-de-verre* technique, chunks of slab glass are set into a matrix of concrete or expoxy (figure 48). Robert Pinart and Jean-Jacques Duval were early proponents of the *dalle-de-verre* technique, popular in the United States after World War II.[38]

Window fabrication, beginning with drawing the cartoon, is done in a glass studio. Today studios are organized and operate according to the traditional model set in the Middle Ages and reestablished in the nineteenth century. Some of the studios presently producing windows have been actively glazing buildings for well over one hundred years. Many of the windows on display in the exhibition and illustrated throughout this catalog have been produced by J & R Lamb Studios, Clifton, New Jersey, founded in 1857 (figures 19, 51, 52);[39] Franz Mayer of Munich, Germany, founded in 1847; Derix Glasstudios, Taunusstein, Germany, founded in 1870 (figure 101);[40] Rohlf's Stained & Leaded Glass, Mount Vernon, New York, founded in 1920 (figures 59, 105, 106, 108, 109); Conrad Schmitt Studios, New Berlin, Wisconsin, founded 1889 (figures 36, 42). Other studios have loaned windows from their collections: Gaytee Stained Glass, Minneapolis, Minnesota, founded in 1918 (figures 29, 30, 32); and Franklin Art Glass Studios, Columbus, Ohio, founded in 1924 (figures 43, 44).

Artist, studio and glassmaker all work together to produce the stained glass windows we see in our churches, synagogues, civic, commercial and residential buildings.

ENDNOTES

1 John G. Hawthorne/ Cyril Stanley Smith, *Theophilus On Divers Arts, the Foremost Medieval Treatise on Painting, Glassmaking and Metalwork* (New York, 1979), 47–48.

2 Ibid., 52–53.

3 Ibid., xxviii. For an overview of the written tradition of glassmaking see: ibid., xxvii-xxxi. For an exhaustive and excellent study of the glassmaking clay tablets excavated in Mesopotamia see: A. Leo Oppenheim et al, *Glass and Glassmaking in Ancient Mesopotamia, An edition of the Cuneiform Texts Which Contain Instructions for Glassmakers With a Catalogue of Surviving Objects* (Corning/New York, 1970). For the dating of the tablets see 4–5, 9.

4 For an excellent explanation of the chemistry of glass see Robert H. Brill, "A Note on the Scientist's Definition of Glass," *Journal of Glass Studies*, IV (1962), 127–138.

5 Pliny, *Natural History with an English Translation in Ten Volumes*, vol. 10, Libri XXXVI-XXXVII, by D.E. Eichholz (Cambridge, 1971), 151. For a discussion of the veracity of Pliny's anecdote concerning the discovery of glassmaking see Anita Engle, "From Myth to Reality, An Intelligent Woman's Guide to Glass History," *Readings in Glass History*, 23 (1991), 9–19.

6 For an overview of the development of glassmaking literature beginning in Antiquity see Cyril Stanley Smith and John G. Hawthorne, "*Mappae Clavicula*, A Little Key to the World of Medieval Techniques, An annotated translation based on a collection of the Selestat and Phillipps-Corning manuscripts, with reproduction of the two manuscripts," *Transactions of the American Philosophical Society*, vol. 64/4 (July 1974), 14, footnote 1 and Madeline H. Caviness, *Stained Glass Windows* (Brepols, 1996), 45–46 and bibliography in footnotes 1–7.

7 Brill, "A Note on the Scientist's Definition of Glass," 131, made this apt analogy.

8 For the last 40 years the Corning Museum of Glass has collected for scientific analysis glasses from various places dating to various centuries under the direction of Dr. Robert H. Brill. Results of the analyses may be found in Robert H. Brill, *Chemical Analyses of Early Glasses*, 2 vols. (Corning, 1999).

9 For a good layman's introduction to the variety of glasses now made and their uses see James E. Hammesfahr/Clair L. Strong, *Creative Glass Blowing* (San Francisco, 1968), 6–14.

10 Brill, "A Note on the Scientist's Definition of Glass," 132–34 and Roy Newton, "The Weathering of Medieval Window Glass," *Journal of Glass Studies*, XVII (1975), 164.

11 Robert H. Brill, "The Scientific Investigation of Ancient Glasses," *Proceedings from the Eighth International Conference on Glass* (London, 1968), 48. For the production of natron in the Middle East and its trade in Europe see Anita Engle, "Luxury Glass of the Roman Period," *Readings in Glass History*, 21 (Jerusalem, 1988), 55–72 .

12 For sources of natron see Engle, "Luxury Glass of the Roman Period," 47–49, 63; for natron production in Egypt, ibid., 66–67.

13 Robert H. Brill, personal communication, April 12, 2002. I am grateful to Dr. Brill for explaining the chemistry of glasses to me.

14 Eraclius, *De Coloribus et Artibus Romanorum*, Book III, chapter VII as quoted in Mary P. Merrifield, *Medieval and Renaissance Treatises on the arts of Painting, Original Texts with English Translations*, (Mineola, 1999), 212. In a footnote to her translation of this passage Merrifield identifies "fania" as beech-wood trees. Engle, "Luxury Glass of the Roman Period," 55 notes the shift in flux in Europe in the Middle Ages.

15 For the use of marine plant ashes, known as *barilla*, in glass making along the Mediterranean Coast see Engle, "Luxury Glass of the Roman Period," 47 and Ruth Hurst Vose, *Glass* (London, 1980), 67.

16 Newton, "The Weathering of Medieval Window Glass," 163 and footnote 19.

17 Smith and Hawthorne, *Mappae Clavicula*, 67.

18 Merrifield, *Medieval and Renaissance Treatises on Painting*, 212–214.

19 Brill, "A Brief Note in the Scientist's Definition of Glass," 134.

20 Personal communication Michael Cuillinane, Bendheim, Clifton, NJ, October 2002.

21 Pliny, *Natural History*, translated by Eichholz, 153.

22 For medieval manufacture of glass see Richard Marks, *Stained Glass in England During the Middle Ages* (Buffalo, 1991), 28–31; Caviness, *Stained Glass Windows*, 46–56.

23 The most striking evidence of this is glass from a thirteenth-century grisaille window from the Château of Rouen discussed by Meredith Lillich, "Three Essays on French Grisaille Glass," *Journal of Glass Studies* 15 (1973), 75. For the use of roundels in architectural glass see H. Weber Wilson, *Great Glass in American Decorative Windows and Doors before 1920* (New York, 1986), 86–87.

24 Hawthorne and Smith, *Theophilus, On Divers Arts*, 57.

25 For a more detailed explanation of annealing see Hammesfahr and Stong, *Creative Glass Blowing*, 134–136.

26 Lamberts Glashütte, Production Brochure, undated, unnumbered.

27 I thank Dan Waber, Kokomo Opalescent Glass, Kokomo, Indiana, for explaining their production methods to me.

28 For the history of Kokomo Opalescent Glass see, Chapter 2, 42 of this catalog.

29 I thank Lorna Lovells, Uroboros Glass Studios, Inc., Portland, Oregon, for explaining their hand rolled glass production with me. The following explanations were based on Uroboros's method of production.

30 Personal communication, Nov. 8, 2002, Steve Zebert, Flabeg Corporation, Brackenridge, PA.

31 Albinus Elskus, *The of Art Painting on Glass, Techniques and Designs for Stained Glass*, (New York, 1980), 3.

32 Merrifield, *Medieval and Renaissance Treatises*, 526–528.

33 For enamel paint see Hammesfahr and Strong, *Creative Glass Blowing*, 162.

34 For examples of Islamic glass with silver stain see Stefano Carboni/David Whitehouse with contributions by Robert H. Brill and William Gudenrath, *Glass of the Sultans* (New York, 2001). For the use of silver stain in medieval windows see Meredith Parsons Lillich, "European Stained Glass around 1300: The Introduction of Silver Stain," in: Liskar, Elisabeth, ed., *Europäische Kunst um 1300*, Akten des XXV. Internationaler Kongresses für Kunstgeschichte, 6 (Vienna, 1986), 45-59.

35 Merrifield, *Medieval and Renaissance Treatises*, 494.

36 Cennino Cennini, *Libro dell'arte. The Craftsman's Handbook: The Italian "Il llibro dell'arte" by Cennino d'Andrea Cennini*, translated by Daniel V. Thompson, Jr. (New York, 1960), 111.

37 Reyntiens, *The Beauty of Stained Glass*, 11.

38 See Chapter 5, 98 of this catalog.

39 For the history of J & R Lamb Studios, see Chapter 2, 43–45 of this catalog. I thank Donald Samick for his generosity with information and loans.

40 I am grateful to Barbara Derix and Irene Moliter, Derix Glasstudios Taunusstein, Germany, for generously supplying many of the glass samples reproduced here.

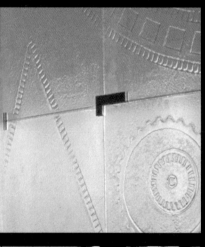

7 FOCUS ARTISTS

DOUGLAS J. HANSEN

AS THE QUALITY AND WAVELENGTH OF LIGHT CHANGES DURING THE COURSE OF THE DAY, OR WITH THE PASSING OF SEASONS, SO THE EFFECT OF THE GLASS CHANGES, ALTERING COLOR VALUES AND PROVIDING ENDLESS VARIATION FOR AN ART SENSITIVE TO THIS PHENOMENON.

Douglas Hansen (1949–) founded Hansen and Associates in 1976 with the purpose of pioneering large-scale fused, leaded, and glued glass. He has also designed standing and aerial sculpture for public and private commissions, including the Ballard Bay Theater and the Keiro Nursing Home, both in Seattle, Washington. In 1997, he worked with Ed Carpenter using translucent, dichroic, and kiln-fused glass for the altar installation of St. Mark's Cathedral in Seattle, Washington, discussed in this catalog. For the Ignatius Chapel (figure 94, 95) he used a complex system of fusing glass of different densities by firing the windows in stages.

Artist's Statement

My medium has been light. I have manipulated this light through the use of architectural glass in many forms: leaded, fused, slumped, painted, glued and sculpted. I have also placed a focus on different light possibilities through the use of fiber optics, LED (light emitting diode) and neon. For structural support I also work with various metals such as stainless steel, aluminum, copper and silver wire. As the quality and wavelength of light changes during the course of the day, or with the passing of seasons, so the effect of the glass changes, altering color values and providing endless variation for an art sensitive to this phenomenon. Glass has become a simple medium for me to form into desired results and is made with attention to safety.

Over the past twenty-seven years I have designed interactive pieces for Percent for Art commissions and recent public and private spaces in Europe as well as many placements in the United States, most recently Alaska's Service High School in Anchorage, Alaska. My goal in projects is to make pieces with constantly changing light and form that inspire the viewer to interact with it in some way, and to give a sense of subtle motion to a space.

Selected Work

2003 Metal and glass arches over pedestrian bridge, City of Wenatchee, Washington (in progress)

2002 Glass wall sculpture, Alaska's Service High School, Anchorage, Alaska

1999 Leaded, glued glass and rock, Tukwila Fire Station, Tukwila, Washington

1989 Cantilevered glass sidewalk and sculpture, U. S. West, Seattle, Washington; Arai/Jackson Architects

1989 Fused glass/free-standing screens, Market Tower, Seattle, Washington; Jim Garrett, Architect

1986 Glass wall, Keiro Nursing Home, Seattle, Washington

CAST GLASS SEEMS TO TRAP
LIGHT WITHIN ITS MATERIAL. ITS TRANSLUCENCY
OR TRANSPARENCY MAINTAINS A GLOW OF
REFLECTED LIGHT, REFRACTED LIGHT, OR THE
LIGHT DISPERSED ON ADJACENT SURFACES.

Steven Holl (1947–) established Steven Holl Architects in New York in 1976. He is an honors graduate of the University of Washington. He studied architecture in Rome in 1970, and did post-graduate work at the Architectural Association in London in 1976. He has been a tenured professor at the Columbia University Graduate School of Architecture and Planning, New York since 1989, and has held teaching positions at the University of Washington, Seattle, Pratt Institute, New York, Parsons School of Design, New York, and the University of Pennsylvania, Philadelphia. A charismatic presence in the classroom, as well as in the studio, Holl was commissioned by Seattle University, a Jesuit school, to design a new chapel, completed in 1996 (figure 14). Widely acclaimed by users and visitors alike, the chapel has won many honors, including both national American Institute of Architects Design and Religious Architecture awards.

Holl investigates concepts of light and space through a practice of making watercolor drawings in a small notebook even before he is fully awake, thus tapping into a free-flow of ideas. The architect has long been engaged in the mystical – indeed his exploration of the nature of forms and sensation, especially light, has been characteristic of all his work. Seattle University believed that through Holl's design, people could experience old rituals – those of the tradition of Ignatius of Loyola and Catholicism – in new ways, looking towards the future rather than the past. Given the religious diversity of the campus, the chapel site was conceived as field, pool, and building, allowing many different kinds of people of varying spiritual backgrounds a space to pause and reflect (figures 14, 96, 97). An extraordinary blending of solids and voids, of ephemeral light and tactile material, Holl's spare but sensuous statement has been heralded as reverential space extraordinarily attuned to urban setting.

Artist's Statement

The chapel is sited to form a new campus quadrangle green space to the north, the west – and in the future, to the east. Directly to the south of the chapel is a reflecting pond or "thinking field." In the Jesuits' "spiritual exercises" no single method is prescribed – "different methods helped different people..."; here a unity of differences gather into one. The light is sculpted by a number of different volumes emerging from the roof. Each of these irregularities aims at different qualities of light:

I. Procession Natural Sunlight
II. Narthex Natural Sunlight
III. Nave Yellow field with blue lens (East), Blue field with yellow lens (West)
IV. Blessed Sacrament Orange field with purple lens
V. Choir Green field with red lens
VI. Reconciliation Chapel Purple field with orange lens
VII. Bell Tower and Pond Projecting, reflecting night light

FIGURE 96

Steven Holl Architects

**Ignatius Chapel
(interior), 1996**

Seattle University,
Seattle, WA

FIGURE 97

**Steven Holl Architects,
Douglas Hansen,
glass artist**

**Ignatius Chapel
(window wall), 1996**

Seattle University,
Seattle, WA

Each light volume corresponds to a part of the program of Jesuit Catholic worship. The south: facing light corresponds to the procession, a fundamental part of the Mass. The city: facing north light corresponds to the Chapel of the Blessed Sacrament and to the mission of outreach to the community. The main worship space has a volume of east and west light. The concept of different lights is further developed in the dialectic combination of a pure colored lens and a field of reflected color within each light volume. A baffle is constructed opposite the large window of each "bottle of light." Each of the baffles is back-painted in a bright color; only the reflected color can be seen from within the chapel. This colored light pulses with life when a cloud passes over the sun. Each bottle combines the reflected color with a colored lens of the complementary color. At night, which is the particular time of gatherings for Mass in this university chapel, the light volumes are like colored beacons shining in all directions out across the campus. On occasions, for those constantly praying, the lights will shine throughout the night. The visual phenomena of complementary colors can be experienced by staring at a blue rectangle and then a white surface. One will see a yellow rectangle; this complementarity contributes to the two-fold merging of concept and phenomena in the chapel.

My choice of glass, fabricated by Douglas Hansen, corresponds to my perception of the material. A sponge can absorb several times its weight in liquid without changing its appearance. Cast glass seems to trap light within its material. Its translucency or transparency maintains a glow of reflected light, refracted light, or the light dispersed on adjacent surfaces. The intermeshing material properties and optic phenomena open a field of exploration. Phenomenal zones likewise open to sound, smell, taste, and temperature as well as to material transformation. All are part of architecture.

Selected Work

CURRENT

Art and Art History Building, University of Iowa.
Iowa City, Iowa

Pratt Instiute, Higgins Hall Center Wing,
Brooklyn, New York

Whitney Waterworks Park, Hamden, Connecticut

2002 Simmons Hall, MIT, Cambridge, Massachusetts

2001 College of Architecture and Landscape
Architecture, University of Minnesota,
Minneapolis, Minnesota

1993 Storefront for Art and Architecture, New York,
New York

Exhibition

1991 Walker Art Center in Minneapolis (solo show):
Architecture Tomorrow, Henry Art Gallery in
Seattle, Washington and in 1992–93 exhibited
throughout Europe

Awards

2000 Progressive Architecture Awards, Nelson-Atkins
Museum of Art, Kansas City, Missouri

1999 New York AIA Design Award, Cranbrook
Institute of Science, Bloomfield Hills, Michigan

1999 National AIA Design Award, Kiasma, The
Museum of Contemporary Art, Helsinki, Finland

1998 National AIA Design Award Chapel of St.
Ignatius, Seattle University, Seattle, Washington

1997 National AIA Religious Architecture Award,
Chapel of St. Ignatius, Seattle University, Seattle,
Washington

1996 AIA award for Design Excellence 190 unit
Makuhari Housing in Chiba, Japan

1995 New York Honor Awards for Excellence in
Design for "Chapel of St. Ignatius" in Seattle,
Washington, and the "Cranbrook Institute of
Science" addition and renovation in Bloomfield
Hills, Michigan

1991 New York City Art Commission Excellence in
Design Award, The Renovation of the Strand
Theater, Brooklyn, New York

1990 Arnold W. Brunner Prize in Architecture,
American Academy and Institute of Arts and
Letters

References

Steven Holl, *Idea and Phenomena* (2002).
—*Written in Water* (2002).
—*Parallax* (New York, 2000).
The Chapel of St. Ignatius (New York, 1999).
"Steven Holl 1996-1999," *El Croquis* (Madrid, 1999).
"Intertwining with the City: Museum of Contemporary
Art in Helsinki," *Harvard Architecture Review* 10 (1998).
Light Constructions (exh. cat.), Museum of Modern Art,
New York, 1995.

Stephen Knapp (1947–) has gained an international reputation for large-scale works of art held in public, corporate, and private collections, in media as diverse as kiln-formed, dichroic, and cast glass, metal, stone, mosaic and ceramic. He frequently writes and lectures on architectural art glass, the collaborative process, and the integration of art and architecture. Knapp's work has appeared in many international publications including *Art & Antiques*, *Architectural Record*, *Honoho Geijutsu*, *Identity*, *Interior Design*, *Interiors*, *Nikkei Architecture*, *Progressive Architecture*, and *The New York Times*.

Stephan Knapp graduated from Hamilton College with a Liberal Arts degree in 1969 and began creating photographic artwork in 1971. By 1975 his relationship with a number of progressive interior designers and architects encouraged him to begin designing large-scale, site-specific photographic installations, such as ceramic murals for USAA Federal Savings Bank in San Antonio, Texas in 1985. Having experimented with new processes as a photographer, in his large-scale work he explored techniques for etching metals and the application of porcelain enamel to steel. By the 1980s, Knapp's installations were encompassing ceramic, etched glass, stainless steel, and mirror surfaces, exemplified by the forty-four foot wall for Harnischfeger Industries in Milwaukee, Wisconsin in 1996 (figure 98). Other installations also included painted stainless steel and painted concrete, demonstrating his versatility with many different materials in new and creative ways.

In the late 1980s he began to focus on work with glass. As a photographer, Knapp saw the possibilities of kiln-formed glass to receive graphic definition. After sketching the full-size cartoon, Knapp often fabricates the molds using a variety of materials whose textures impact the finished product. His art testifies to a strong direction in contemporary work – the artistic response to technical advancements that encourage new forms. Knapp's work for *Reflections on Glass* is site-specific, designed for The Gallery at the American Bible Society and so unavailable for photography for this catalog. An example of his work can be seen in *Stories from Light – told and untold – a Continuous Journey*, created in 2001 for the Women and Babies Hospital of Lancaster General, Lancaster, Pennsylvania (figure 99). The twenty-six foot circular installation of dichroic glass and stainless steel exploits different light sources to create constantly varying patterns of color within the space.

Artist's Statement

My response to glass came as a result of a continuing affair with light. Even in seemingly non-responsive media such a steel, stone, and ceramic, I was attracted to the possibilities of their kinetic response to light. The inherent mystery of glass – this frozen liquid that is neither solid nor fluid – with its uncanny ability to capture energy and release it in response to the viewer's interaction with the object and light, is part of my fascination. Working in

FIGURE 98

Stephen Knapp

Kiln-formed Glass Walls, 1996

Harnischfeger Industries, Milwaukee, WI

FIGURE 99
Stephen Knapp
*Stories from Light –
told and untold – a
Continuous Journey,
2001*
Women and Babies
Hospital, Lancaster
General, Lancaster, PA

kiln-formed glass gives me an opportunity to further engage an audience. The detail in relief in glass draws in viewers and invites them to spend more time with the actual object, to study the content, and to marvel at the changes in the surface with the changes in light, time of day and the passing viewer.

Robert Rauschenberg and Isamu Noguchi have been perhaps my biggest influences. Rauschenberg is important for his assemblages and collages that borrow heavily on imagery and reassembly. When I worked in Japan at Otsuka Ohmi to create some of the largest glass glaze ceramic murals in the world, I was able to see work Rauschenberg had created in the factory shortly before I arrived. I admire Noguchi for the spare nature of his sculpture – the elegant gesture that says that simplicity and beauty has a place in the art world. So much is made of the tortured thinking of the artist, and yet Noguchi was willing to work a piece until it seemed a simple gesture at best. Of the stained glass artists, Johannes Schreiter still remains my favorite, with his strong sense of design and willingness to experiment. There is a touch and sensitivity in his work in glass that I find in no other.

My projects are always the result of dialogues – with the architect, with the committee or commissioning agency, with the community, and with the architecture itself. It is always a give and take, a process of discovery and exploration. Research

forms a key element of my work – both in materials research, and in the project itself – discovering the fabric of the community where the art is going to be placed. Developing pieces evocative of a rich past and hinting at future possibilities is part of many of my projects. My ideal client is one who is both demanding and knowledgeable, willing to get involved and react to the work, without actually wanting to create or totally dictate the direction of the work.

One of my most satisfying projects to date has been the *Crystal Quilt* of 2001 for the Love Library at the University of Nebraska-Lincoln (figure 100). I was not only pleased by the project for such a well-traveled public space, but felt a sense of accomplishment in pushing the medium to include unusually detailed imagery highly appreciated by the viewers. Equally important and satisfying, for a very different reason, is *Stories from Light* at the Women and Babies Hospital in Lancaster, Pennsylvania (figure 99). I was approached to do a stained glass ceiling for a rotunda in the hospital. After viewing the space with the architect, I proposed, and ultimately completed, a sculptural light painting, using dichroic glass, stainless steel, cables, and light.

I think the future of architectural art glass in the twenty-first century will be both varied and widespread. In an increasingly tumultuous world, the hand of the artist will play an even greater role. Light, with its manifest ability to heal and affect moods, will drive the inclusion of glass in even more projects. Architectural art glass will grow from the traditional forms of stained glass to painted float glass, kiln-formed and cast-glass walls, and a host of new possibilities.

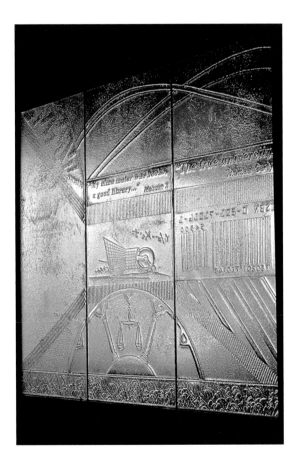

FIGURE 100
Stephen Knapp
Crystal Quilt, **2001**
Love Library, University
of Nebraska-Lincoln
Lincoln, NE

Selected Work

Kiln-formed Glass

2002   Congregation of Sisters of St. Agnes, Fond du Lac, Wisconsin; Envision, Fond du Lac, Wisconsin; DesignWorks Studio, Lenexa, KA

2001   The New Doors and Southwick, Hoffman and Friends, Worcester Public Library, Worcester, Massachusetts; Tappé Associates, Architects

2001   Crystal Quilt, Love Library University of Nebraska-Lincoln, Lincoln, Nebraska; The Clark Enersen Partnership, Architects

1997   Dana Farber Cancer Institute, Boston, Massachusetts; Rothman Partners Inc., Architects

1996   Kiln-formed glass entry wall, Harnischfeger Industries, Milwaukee, Wisconsin; Kahler-Slater, Architects

Light Sculptures

2001   *Stories from Light - told and untold - a Continuous Journey*, Women and Babies Hospital of Lancaster General, Lancaster, Pennsylvania; IKM Architects

2000   *Sculptural Light Painting*, Worcester Medical Center, Worcester, Massachusetts; Gene Collins, Euthenics

Mixed Media/Other

2000   The Healing Arts Suite, The Florida Department of Health; Barnett Fronczak Architects and Rolland, DeValle & Bradley, Architects

1999   The Walter Reed Army Institute of Research, Silver Spring, Maryland; HLW Architects

1996   Menorah Medical Center, Kansas City, Missouri; Tranin Design Associates, Architects

References

Stephen Knapp, *The Art of Glass: Integrating Architecture and Glass* (Gloucester 1998).
Andrew Moor, *Architectural Glass Art* (New York, 1997).

Linda Lichtman (1941–) first acquired a Bachelor's and then a Master's Degree in Social work from Simmons College, Boston, before turning to art. In the early 1960s she took classes in glass, discovering *The Technique of Stained Glass* by Patrick Reyntiens. In 1973, she studied with Reyntiens at Burleighfield House in Buckinghampshire, England, an international school for artists. At the Massachusetts College of Art, Boston, she earned a B.F.A. in Painting in 1974. From 1974–76 she attended the School of the Museum of Fine Arts, Boston, where she studied drawing and architectural stained glass. She has been highly active in glass design, with representation in many public arts commissions.

Her work for the Charter Oak State College, New Britain, Connecticut (figure 101) demonstrates her ability to conceive both form and symbol within an architectural setting. The panels work as a wall, but also evoke the growth of a tree, the most recognizable image being that of the oak leaf, *quercus alba*, labeled as such, in the keystone position. The spontaneity of Lichtman's gesture suggests the spontaneity of the movement of leaves; her choice of colors the change of seasons. Painterly imagery inspired by nature provides a human connection and environment for the viewer. In the *Light Garden* for the Dana Farber Cancer Center in Boston (figure 102), Lichtman positioned stained glass throughout the two clinics as "glowing windows of light." The glass provides a ubiquitous theme, from raised coves in elevator lobbies and waiting areas, to wayfinding markers at hallway corners, to sidelights at conference and procedure room doorways. At the same time, each site has its own program and conditions to which the glass responds. The linear accelerator room has vivid backlit panels to draw the eye through the entry maze and divert the attention of patients in the high-tech machine. Glass inserts into partition screens around waiting areas create colorful patterns with a reflective glint, to engage waiting patients. *Light Garden* is based on the concept that the physical environment is a material expression – a re-statement – of the caring that is given by the Dana Farber Cancer Institute to its patients. The artwork is designed to energize the patients, to engage them in the artwork.

Artist's Statement

Stained glass windows have a special meaning for me, as they are the expressive boundaries between an interior, personal world and the exterior. They are permeable yet somehow impregnable, expressive yet anonymous. Stained glass connects us to and separates us from the world. It reveals and conceals. It protects and exposes. It creates a seemingly fragile boundary that touches both the material and the immaterial. Although an artist always works with deliberation, intent, and vision, the glass remains somewhat autonomous. It is like a child sent into the world, of my shaping but independent of me.

Some artists elicited a strong response in me

the first time I ever saw their work, among them the German Expressionists – Egon Schiele, Oskar Kokoschka, Max Beckmann, Emil Nolde and Paul Klee – and stained glass artists Harry Clarke of Ireland and Hans von Stockhausen of Germany. I admire medieval stained glass (twelfth and thirteenth centuries) for its dramatic abstract qualities and simplicity. Post-war German stained glass exemplifies for me successful stained glass in secular architecture. Personal contact with some of the German artists, as well as my friendships with Irish and Welsh stained glass artists, has been very important. I feel indebted to Patrick Reyntiens, my first teacher in glass and an inspiring person. Paul Marioni, with whom I studied in 1974, and Stephen Taylor, an English artist now working in New Zealand were also important teachers.

For architectural commissions, I strive to understand the programmatic needs of the users, and the site/architecture without allowing the client to have undue influence. This is a delicate balance. After much "absorption" of information from these sources from the outside, I work on my own for some time. I need distance from the client while working on conceptual designs. I often offer two or three options to the client, depending upon my feelings about the designs. Oddly, it's the public art projects that allow me the most autonomy. Although dealing with bureaucracies and project managers can often be challenging, I can strive to do the work for the kinds of civic buildings and "audiences" which interest me the most. Thus, I seek work in buildings such as hospitals, courthouses, schools, fire stations, and airports, rather than in residential settings. My ideal client speaks with one voice, and doesn't change goals as the project develops, and is as passionate about his or her work and mission as I am about mine.

My most satisfying project was for the Dana Farber Cancer Institute in Boston. Titled *Light Garden*, this glass artwork is integrated throughout the Radiation Oncology and Nuclear Medicine clinics. A total of twenty-eight sites are involved, with as many as thirty-two stained glass panels in each site. The major design challenge of this project was to make an inviting, patient-friendly environment in a sub-basement, devoid of natural light. Color, light, texture and movement in the work contribute to the feeling of the lifeforce being activated, and inspiring hope (figure 102).

In the coming century, I think stained glass will be used much more frequently in secular settings, as will all architectural artwork. More techniques for manipulating color, light, transparency, and other qualities will become available and dedicated fabrication businesses (studios) that cater to the stained glass artists will become available in this country as they have been in Europe. The quality of stained glass artwork will be enhanced, which will increase demand significantly. There should be the equivalent of the Nobel, Pulitzer or Oscar for the greatest new stained glass window each year.

Selected Works

2003 Logan Airport MBTA Station, Boston, Massachusetts (in progress)

2002 Hitchner Hall Biology Building, University of Maine, Orono, Maine
Lewiston District, Courthouse, Lewiston, Maine

2001 The Connecticut State University System Headquarters, Hartford, Connecticut
Long Lane School, Connecticut Juvenile Training Facility, Middleton, Connecticut

2000 Dana Farber Cancer Institute, Memorial Wall Sculpture, Boston, Massachusetts

1999 Charter Oak State College, New Britain, Connecticut

1998 Dana Farber Cancer Institute, Nuclear Medicine & Radiation Oncology, Boston, Massachusetts

1993 New England Journal of Medicine, Editiorial Office, Harvard University Medical School, Countway Library, Boston, Massachusetts

1991 Coolidge Corner Library, Brookline, Massachusetts

Exhibitions

2001 Artist & Architect Collaboration, Maud Morgan Visual Arts Center, Cambridge, Massachusetts

1998 Linda Lichtman, Cochrane Gallery, London, Great Britain

1997 Traces of Travel, Crawford Municipal Art Gallery, Cork, Ireland, and Glass Art Gallery, London, Great Britain

1996 The Eighth Triennial, Fuller Museum of Art, Brockton, Massachusetts

1992 Structures & Images (solo), Trustman Art Gallery, Simmons College, Boston, Massachusetts

1993 The Glass Canvas, Curator and Exhibitor, Society of Arts and Crafts, Boston, Massachusetts

1994 Transforming Transparency, Art Complex Museum, Duxbury, Massachusetts

1989 International Flatglass, 36 Women From 12 Countries, Germany and France

Visiting Artist

Central Saint Martin's College of Art, London, Great Britain; Swansea Institute, Swansea, Wales, Great Britain; Rhode Island School of Design, Providence, Rhode Island; Massachusetts College of Art, Boston, Massachusetts; School of the Museum of Fine Arts, Boston, Massachusetts

FIGURE 103
Linda Lichtman
Unity Windows **(detail), 2001**
Long Lane School, Connecticut Juvenile Training Facility
Middletown, CT

Ellen Mandelbaum (1938–) graduated from Indiana University, Bloomington, Indiana with a Bachelor of Arts in 1960, followed by a Master of Fine Arts in painting in 1963. She studied architectural glass design at the Pilchuck School, Washington in 1983 and 1984. Both her autonomous panels and architectural work have been exhibited internationally. Susan Beeh-Lustenberger, associated with the Hessisches Landesmuseum, Darmstadt, Germany has credited Mandelbaum with working in "a direction that started one of the most important trends in contemporary stained glass today" – her insistence on painterly expression and the retention of the brush stroke, linking the applied art of glass with the fine art of painting.

Mandelbaum is a painter working with glass. She explains that "traditionally artists divide glass painting into matting and tracing, first creating a thin line, then putting down a general tone. I do them together, which is a little more like regular painting in a way. I love to put down a tone and blend using a wide brush: then I scratch through and release the light." Andrew Moor characterizes Mandelbaum's work as "one of the finest examples of abstract expressionism." Her brushwork is richly gestural and the window combines both the spontaneity and the solidity of architectural forms. Two of Mandelbaum's recent commissions for sacred spaces show her characteristic style: the windows for the Adath Jeshurun Synagogue in Minnetonka, Minnesota (figure 104) and those for Marian Woods

convent in Hartsdale, New York (figure 105, 106). The windows for the Adath Jeshurun Synagogue, which received a Religious Art Award from the American Institute of Architects, represent the Minyan (ten worshippers needed for prayer) (figure 104). The continuous reamy (glass with a fluid, watery texture) glass design, which flows from left to right, was inspired by the river of light that Abraham saw. The jury stated that the " … abstract feeling (is) nonetheless evocative of traditional stained glass (…) You can see the lake views become part of the aesthetic." Like the work of Mark Gulsrud, also represented in this catalog, she creates brilliant intersections of representation and reality, allowing clear glass to bring the view of natural landscape into the image.

The glass for the chapel at Marian Woods, like the windows in the Adath Jeshurun Synagogue, integrates the wooded landscape with the image. The handmade art glass changes with the light of day and with the trees changing in season. Mandelbaum notes that Marian Woods was an ideal client: "The sisters and liturgical consultant were wonderful; their idea to integrate the glass art with the woods was close to my heart."

Artist's Statement
As a painter in oil and watercolor, I discovered in glass a new, exciting medium full of rich potential. The wall of glass samples from my supplier, S.A.

FIGURE 104

Ellen Mandelbaum

Fabricated by Keith Studios

Minyan Windows, 1995

Adath Jeshurun Synagogue, Minnetonka, MN

FIGURE 105

Ellen Mandelbaum

Fabricated by Rohlf's Stained & Leaded Glass

Marian Woods Chapel (interior view), 2001

Hartsdale, NY

Bendheim in New York, seemed to present color expanded by texture, degree of translucency, beyond anything I had seen. As I worked I imagined that the different colors of glass were arranged like colors on a palette. Painting on glass allowed fluent gesture, tone, and drawing that could break outside the lead lines. I still look to painters for inspiration, the Dutch seventeenth-century masters Vermeer and Rembrandt for their depiction of light, and for color, the French twentieth-century artist, Matisse. All of the avant-garde movements that I was aware of had each claimed exclusive ownership of the truth and I had learned not to take anyone at face value. I saw art as richer, warmer, and more inclusive but I did come to see Modernism as a tool for my personal expression. I also learned from the study of artists in glass, especially Ludwig Schaffrath, Albinas Elskus, Jochem Poensgen, and Ed Carpenter.

I always hope to work with the architect and client to take in their needs and vision. By beginning the commission through watercolor, what I still believe is my most natural medium, I keep my personal vision fresh. My mother taught me to paint with watercolors when I was seven or eight.

Landscape, which I still sketch in watercolor, has been a constant inspiration. As I designed more and more windows, I saw that glass helped to define the environment and I ultimately came to incorporate the view of environment in the glass. The results in windows have often been characterized as "serene," although my commissions have varied greatly: a lobby for an infertility center in the Greater Baltimore Medical Center, a synagogue chapel in Minnesota, or a monumental glass wall for the South Carolina Aquarium.

I have never been cynical but have always thought of art as good. It's very satisfying to think about the service or usefulness of the artwork. I believe that art can be healing but it is not just a question of color, form, and light, or even subject matter. It is also a question of balance and harmony and wholeness, and even of my intentions and feeling as I work.

For the future of the twenty-first century I wonder if it may be difficult to maintain the technique of leaded glass. Many architects and designers prefer a technique without a dark edge. It might be nice in some cases but leaded glass is actually the most natural way to use the many different colors of the most beautiful handmade glass. It is also strong and permanent. I hope that the new techniques being developed understand what has always made leaded windows great.

Selected Works

2001 Marian Woods, Hartsdale, New York

2000 South Carolina Aquarium, Charleston, South Carolina

1998 McKnight Memorial Window, Community Church, New York, New York

1993 Two painted panels for Greater Baltimore Medical Center Hospital Women's Center Lobby, Townsend, Maryland

Awards

2001 Ministry and Liturgy, Bene & Best of Show (First Prize): 1998 Christ United Methodist Church, Honolulu, Hawaii

1997 American Institute of Architects, IFRAA Religious Art Award of Excellence: 1995 Adath Jeshurun Synagogue, Minnetonka, Minnesota

Exhibitions

1998 Painting and Glass Art (solo), Queens College Art Center, Flushing, New York

References

"An Artist's Statement: A Solo Exhibition (Work of Ellen Mandelbaum at the Benjamin S. Rosenthal Library)," *Stained Glass* 93 (Summer 1998): 122–25.

Christopher Peterson, *The Art of Stained Glass* (Gloucester, 1998).

Andrew Moor, *Architectural Glass Art* (New York, 1997).

Ellen Mandelbaum, "Synagogue with a View," *Stained Glass* 90 (Winter 1995): 314–16.

"Interrupted Waterfall," *Stained Glass* 88 (Spring 1993): 30.

Ellen Mandelbaum, "In My House There Are Many Mansions," *Faith & Forum* (Spring 1981): 37–38.

FIGURE 106

Ellen Mandelbaum

Fabricated by Rohlf's Stained & Leaded Glass

Mystic Rose Window, 2001

Marian Woods Chapel, Hartsdale, NY

Ellen Miret (1954–) attended the University of New Mexico, Albuquerque; Pima Community College, Tucson, Arizona; and the School of Visual Arts, New York City. She has felt at home designing for a variety of clients – Catholic, Protestant, Jewish – and has executed large and small scale and figural as well as abstract work. She exhibits an unusual grace for scale, given the windows' placement and shape. For her award-winning entrance window for the Bergen Highland's Methodist Church, she combined the long triangular shape with an abstracted image of the Methodist flame and cross rising in the center. The subtle coloration of teal, aubergine, gold, and pale blue gives the sensation of floating, liberated shapes. Designed to be seen in transmitted or reflected light, the entrance makes a welcoming statement when looked upon from afar. Her vertical windows on the theme of music for Christ Church in Bronxville, New York are more densely packed, with expressionist energies of the leadlines forming a strong graphic amidst layered forms. The artist's work for the Ascension Mausoleum in Monsey, New York is on a very large scale, combining figural and architectural shapes.

Miret's challenge was to integrate traditional iconography into a highly explicit architectural frame. In the example of the Mausoleum Chapel at Monsey, there is a square (Greek) cross design,

FIGURE 107
Ellen Miret

Harley Ellington Pierce Yee Associates, Architects

Ascension Mausoleum (overall view), 1990

Archdiocese of New York, Monsey, NY

FIGURE 108

Ellen Miret

**Fabricated by Rohlf's
Stained & Leaded Glass**

Christ of the Ascension,
1990

Ascension Mausoleum

Archdiocese of
New York, Monsey, NY

emphasizing the window wall at each end of the arms of the cross (figure 107). The windows were conceived to rise up over the surrounding structures and at night to also function as murals. The *Ascension of Christ*, returning transfigured to the Father, stands as the pivotal image of God's promise to believers (figure 108) . Over the altar, which is fitted with a sculpted crucifix, Miret placed two energetic angels blowing trumpets to call the dead to arise (figure 109). Opposite them is Christ ascending on a cloud and on the two flanking walls, the Virgin Mary and St. Joseph. Joseph's staff flowers and the

FIGURE 109
Ellen Miret

**Fabricated by Rohlf's
Stained & Leaded Glass**

Angels of the Resurrection,
1990

Ascension Mausoleum

Archdiocese of New York,
Monsey, NY

Virgin holds the lily of the Annunciation, each image set within the lower, more earth-bound part of the window. Christ's figure, however, ascends to break through the circle, as do the angels, already penetrating the realm of heaven. The geometric pattern of the window opens up to emphasize Christ and the angels and the cross shape inherent in the architectural frame.

Artist's Statement

Often too much is said about visual art – the work should be able to engage the viewer without an explanation. There are so many different ways to look at the same image and I don't want to limit anyone's interpretation or response. I did a memorial for a family that included an angel's feet and legs climbing Jacob's Ladder. Accompanying the angel was a bird that I intended as a visual metaphor for words to the departed, "away like a bird to your nest you will fly." When my client saw the full size model, she started to cry and felt that it was her son's feet on the ladder. That was fine with me. Her interpretation meant more than anything I had to say about it.

From the time I was first introduced to glass in high school by my art teacher Mrs. Jensen (who made lamps and thought it would be a viable medium to teach us), I felt that I would design glass for houses of worship. I was definitely not religious as a teenager and young adult, but grew into my spirituality.

I feel fortunate to have worked in a large studio early in my career because it exposed me to many different glass artists from another generation, each with different styles. It also made me comfortable working on such a large scale. Benoit Gilsoul was an influence for me visually in the glass world. Per Bergathon and Fredrick Cole were very supportive. Lou Bunin, film maker and master puppeteer, was a mentor/influence as well as my father, Gil Miret, another amazing artist. Twentieth-century painters like Pablo Picasso, Henry Matisse, and Paul Cézanne, and the Cubists interest me – also Jackson Pollock, Mark Rothko. Anslem Kieffer made an impression many years ago, as did Lucien Freud. I like to look at ancient art of all kinds and medieval glass and African art. I like to look at everything, really.

In working on a new commission, the first thing I like to do is to meet with a large number of the intended audience to listen. Then I think about things for a while, sometimes a month or so before I start to draw. Afterwards, it is best to meet with the small group of decision-makers for practical implementation and a design contract. I do not like the practice of working on speculation. I don't think it's fair, and other fields don't. The perfect client would come to me before the building was finished and after reviewing many artists' work (including mine) and educating themselves in the medium by seeing a lot of installations. They would trust (because they have seen my work) that I will do the best job that I possibly can.

I think my work is a gift and I am thankful for it. It is hard to pick a favorite commission but what stands out for the process and the interaction is Beth Israel in Uwchland, Pennsylvania. I was brought in by the architect Michael Callori while it was still on paper. He and I have worked on many projects together since 1982. I was able to design the glass and also the temple furnishings of the Arc, Lamp, and a memorial. The space, open and inviting, has continuity. The Ascension Mausoleum was very satisfying. Balancing the light was a challenge, along with the enormous scale and combination of geometric and figural work, all in lead.

Stained glass in the twenty-first century? – I hope stained glass continues to grow out of its architectural foundations, evolving as architecture evolves but never losing sight of its ancient connection as a vehicle of sacred expression in relationship to sacred space.

Selected Works

2001 Marist College, Poughkeepsie, New York

2000 Beth Shalom, Teaneck, New Jersey, Michael Callori Architect

1999 St. Aloysius Church, New Caanan, Connecticut; Henry Menzies Architect

1997 St. Mary's Church, Portland, Connecticut; Pierz Architects

1996 Temple Beth Israel, Uwchland, Pennsylvania; Michael Callori Architect

1996 St. Mary's Church, Richmond Township, Pennsylvania; Architectural Studio

1995 Christ Church, Episcopal, Bronxville, New York

1993 Temple Beth El, Cherry Hill, New Jersey; Michael Callori Architect

1992 St. Elizabeth's Church Wyckoff, New Jersey

1991 Ferncliff Mausoleum, Hartsdale, New York, ongoing

1986 Beth El Zedeck, Indianapolis, Indiana

1985 Temple Beth-Orr, Coral Springs, Florida

1985 St. Charles Borromeo, Arlington, Virginia

1984 U.S. Naval Base, Reykjavik, Iceland

1984 St. Joan of Arc, Toledo, Ohio

Awards

1998 Modern Liturgy (Best of Show): 1993 Bergen Highlands Methodist Church, Upper Saddle River, New Jersey; Michael Callori Architect

1986 IFRAA, award for excellence in design

References

Hoover, Richard L. "Transition to Glass," *Stained Glass* (Spring 1991): 34–39.

Miret, Ellen. "Arts that Heal, Words and Images to Move the Spirit and Awaken the Soul," *Glass Arts Magazine* 17/6 (Sept./Oct. 2002): 20–25.

A 1961 graduate of the Middlesborough College of Art (Middlesborough, Yorkshire, Great Britain), David Wilson (1941–) completed post-graduate studies at the Central School of Arts and Crafts, London in 1962. In 1963 he moved to New York City to work at the Rambusch Decorating Company, eventually becoming head of the stained glass department. In 1978 he purchased a twenty-acre property in upstate New York where he moved his studio. Admired for his successful collaborations with architects on large-scale works for both public and private buildings, Wilson pursues the goal of designing glass that adds to and enriches architecture. By emphasizing the importance of visual harmony in the built environment, he creates designs that are the result of reducing forms to their simplest solution.

Wilson's characteristic work is in the tradition of the medieval grisaille window. Grisaille, or predominantly uncolored windows, was the glazing of choice for twelfth-century craftsman monks such as the Cistercians. Utilizing complex interlace and carpet designs, these grisaille windows filled monasteries in France, Germany, and England. The thirteenth century saw a continued interest in the grisaille technique as builders and artisans began to couple the tapestry-like designs with the banded window, as an increased ratio of window-to-wall space became more fashionable. The axial chapel of Auxerre Cathedral and the transept show such interaction (see figure 6). Wilson uses broad areas of color as well, exemplified in his evocation of earth and sky for the Beth David Reform Congregation in 1996 (figure 110).

Wilson uses a carefully selected gamut of glass finely calibrated to carry out his graphic systems. Like much art in the Modernist tradition, the slightest miscalculation of proportion or density can rupture the harmony. Recently, Wilson has incorporated dichroic glass into many compositions. The fine accents enhance the kinetic effect. In the Rehm Library of the Center for Religion, Ethics, and Culture, the College of the Holy Cross, Worcester, Massachusetts, the entrance wall and windows include densely packed, small beveled squares interspersed with dichroic accents that act as prisms for the changing light (figures 111, 112). For this space that houses sacred texts from the world's religions, tall windows construct a scintillating environment. The windows contain mouth-blown antique French and German glass, as well as beveled glass. Interior light is further transferred through the entrance wall, created for the two-story atrium space outside the library, generating an ever-changing color-flecked experience.

Artist's Statement

The possibility of working for a family-related glass art studio in New York City led me to specialize in stained glass while still at the Middlesborough College of Art. This specialization became a fascination. In New York, working for Rambusch Studios,

FIGURE 110
David Wilson
Creation Window, 1996
Beth David Reform
Congregation,
Gladwyne, PA

I continued to explore the medium and I also met many people whose work I admire. I had become aware of the work of Robert Sowers through his book *The Lost Art* while at the Middlesborough College of Art. Later, in New York City, I met Sowers and we became personal friends. I was also influenced by an exhibition of glass panels from various Frank Lloyd Wright houses at the Richard Feigen Gallery on Greene Street. This was an eye-opener.

I have worked with a wide variety of clients, but I see a similar process in the development of projects. I hope to create a reciprocal exchange that is a delicate balance requiring a mutual respect for the integrity of all involved: architect, artist, site, and its users. I most often work through a series of meetings and conversations, which first develop a design "program," leading to a preliminary design,

then a final design. It is a collaborative process. These final designs are then full-sized, fabricated, and installed. The exception to this is competitions, mostly in the public art sector, where the artist goes with his or her intuition about what would be best. The percentage of "wins" is small and there is no opportunity for a collaborative process. I am not sure that there is such a thing as an ideal client – perhaps someone with a super abundance of cash and no preconceived notions as to the end result.

As far as my favorite commission is concerned, it is always the next or current project that is the most satisfying for its challenge and promise. I find myself alive in the absorption of the creative process. Once a project is installed you start to look at it carefully and wonder why you made this or that decision.

As to the future of the medium, I see new artists and designers appearing all the time. I see the art and craft of stained glass capable of endless reinvention. In fact, this reinvention of an ancient and traditional process along with the manipulation of light is the root of my love for this medium.

Selected Work

2002 Spirit of Christ Catholic Church, Arvada, Colorado; Bill Beard/Richard Smith, Architects, Center for Religion, Ethics and Culture, College of the Holy Cross, Worcester, Massachusetts; Graham Gund, Architects
NEC Monorail Station, Newark Airport, Newark, New Jersey; Port Authority of New York and New Jersey

FIGURE 111
David Wilson
Rehm Library windows, 2001–02
College of the Holy Cross, Worcester, MA

2000 Corning Incorporated, New York, New York;
Kevin Roche John Dinkeloo & Associates,
Architects

1999 Sellinger Hall School of Business, Loyola College
in Maryland, Baltimore, Maryland; Bohlin
Cywinski Jackson, Architects

1998 First United Methodist Church, Waynesville,
North Carolina; Atkin Olshin Lawson-Bell,
Architects

1996 Beth David Reform Congregation, Gladwyne,
Pennsylvania; Shapiro Petrauskas Gelber,
Architects.

1994 Le Moyne College Chapel, Syracuse, New York;
Quinlivan Pierik & Krause, Architects

1989 St. Augustine of Canterbury Church, Franklin
Park, New Jersey; Gatarz Venezia, Architects

1998 Washington Hebrew Congregation, Washington
DC; Giorgio Cavaglieri, Architect.

1984 Emanuel Synagogue, West Hartford,
Connecticut; T. Handler Associates, Architects

1983 Murray Weigel Hall Chapel, Fordham University,
Bronx, New York; Martin Holub, Architect

Awards

1999 GSA Design Award, Citation, Washington DC:
1998, U.S. Courthouse and Federal Building,
Charleston WV; Skidmore, Owings & Merrill,
Architects

1994 AIA Religious Art Award, Orlando Fl: 1992,
Reorganized Church of Latter-Day Saints, Temple
& World Headquarters, Independence, MO;
Hellmuth, Obata and Kassabaum Architects

1990 IFRAA Honor Award for Design, Boston,
Massachusetts: 1989, Mary, Mother of the
Church Chapel, National Conference of Catholic
Bishops, Washington DC; Leo Daly, Architects

1987 Award for Excellence in Design, St. George Public
Library, Mayor Koche /Art Commission, New York
City

1984 Award for Excellence in Religious Art, Municipal
Art Society, New York City, Christ the King,
Dunbar, West Virginia

References

Andrew Moor, *Architectural Glass Art* (New York, 1997).
Sydney Lancaster Waller, "The Figure in Leaded Glass,"
Stained Glass 84 (Spring 1989): 25–32.
Christina Neff, "Weaving with Light: The Glass Art of David
Wilson," *E & A Environment & Art Letter* (April 2000): 204-
8, 215

FIGURE 112
David Wilson
Rehm Library windows,
2001–02
College of the Holy
Cross, Worcester, MA

SELECTED BIBLIOGRAPHY

Adams, Henry and others, *John La Farge* (New York, 1986).

Arnold, Hugh, *Stained Glass of the Middle Ages in England and France* (repr. London, 1913).

Brisac, Catherine, *A Thousand Years of Stained Glass* (New York, 1986).

Brown, Sarah, *Stained Glass: An Illustrated History* (New York, 1992).

Clarke, Brian (ed.), *Architectural Stained Glass* (London, 1979).

Connick, Charles J., *Adventures in Light and Color* (New York, 1937).

Duncan, Alastair/Martin Eidelberg/Neil Harris, *Masterworks of Louis Comfort Tiffany* (New York, 1989).

Frueh, Erne R./Florence Frueh, *Chicago Stained Glass* (Chicago, 1983).

Koch, Robert, Louis C. Tiffany, *Rebel in Glass* (New York, 1982).

Lee, Lawrence/George Seddon/Francis Stephens, *Stained Glass* (New York, 1976).

Lloyd, John Gilbert, *Stained Glass in America* (Jenkintown, 1963).

McKean Hugh F., *The Lost Treasures of Louis Comfort Tiffany* (New York, 1980).

Moor, Andrew, *Architectural Glass: A Guide for Design Professionals* (New York, 1989).

Moor, Andrew, *Architectural Glass Art: Form and Technique in Contemporary Glass* (New York, 1997).

Pfaff, Konrad, *Ludwig Schaffrath* (Krefeld, 1977).

Raguin, Virginia C., *Glory in Glass, Stained Glass in the United States: Origins, Variety, and Preservation* (New York: American Bible Society, 1998).

Reyntiens, Patrick, *The Beauty of Stained Glass* (Boston, 1990).

Rigan, Otto B., *New Glass* (San Francisco, 1976).

Schaffrath, Ludwig, *Stained Glass + Mosaic* (Krefeld, 1977).

Sowers, Robert, *Rethinking the Forms of Visual Expression* (Berkley/Los Angeles, 1990).

Sowers, Robert. "New Stained Glass in Germany" *Craft Horizons* 29 (May-June, 1969) 14–21,69.

Sowers, Robert, *The Language of Stained Glass* (Forest Grove, 1981).

Sowers, Robert, *Stained Glass an Architectural Art* (New York, 1965).

Sowers, Robert, *The Lost Art: A Survey of One Thousand Years of Stained Glass* (London, 1954).

Stephany, Erich, *Licht, Glas, Farbe* (Aachen, 1982).

Sturm, James L., *Stained Glass from Medieval Times to the Present: Treasures to be Seen in New York* (New York, 1982).

Tutag, Nola, *Discovering Stained Glass in Detroit* (Detroit, 1987).

Westlake, N. H. J., *A History of Design in Painted Glass* (4 vol.) (London, 1881).

TECHNIQUE:

Bray, Charles, *Dictionary of Glass: Materials and Techniques* (Philadelphia, 1995).

Brill, Robert H., "A Note on the Scientist's Definition of Glass," *Journal of Glass Studies*, IV (1962), 127–138.

__, "The Scientific Investigation of Ancient Glasses," Proceedings from the Eighth International Conference on Glass (London, 1968), 47-68.

__, *Chemical Analyses of Early Glasses*, 2 vols. (Corning, 1999).

Caviness, Madeline H., *Stained Glass Windows* (Brepols, 1996).

Carbino, Stefano/ Whitehouse, David with contributions by Robert H. Brill and William Gudenrath, *Glass of the Sultans* (New York, 2001).

Cennino Cennini, *Libro dell'arte. The craftsman's handbook: the Italian "Il libro dell'arte" by Cennino d'Andrea Cennini*, translated by Daniel V. Thompson, Jr. (New York, 1960).

Duthie, Arthur L., *Decorative Glass Processes* (repr. New York, 1982; orig. publ. in New York, 1911).

Elskus, Albinas, *The Art of Painting on Glass: Techniques and Designs for Stained Glass* (New York, 1980).

Engle, Anita, "Luxury Glass of the Roman Period," *Readings in Glass History*, no. 21 (Jerusalem, 1988).

__, *From Myth to Reality, An Intelligent Woman's Guide to Glass History, Readings in Glass History*, no. 23 (Jerusalem 1991).

Hammesfahr, James E/ Strong, Clair L., *Creative Glass Blowing* (San Francisco, 1968).

Hawthorne, John G./Stanely Smith, Cyril, *Theophilus on Divers Arts, The Foremost Medieval Treatise on Painting, Glassmaking and Metalwork* (New York, 1979).

Hurst Vose, Ruth, *Glass* (London, 1980).

Lillich, Meredith, "Three Essays on French Grisaille Glass," *Journal of Glass Studies* 15 (1973), 69–78.

Marks, Richard, *Stained Glass in England During the Middle Ages* (Toronto, 1991).

Merrifield, Mary P., *Medieval and Renaissance Treatises on the Arts of Painting*, Original Texts with English Translations (Mineola/New York, 1999).

Newton, Roy "The Weathering of Medieval Window Glass," *Journal of Glass Studies*, XVII (1975), 161–168.

Pliny, *Natural History with an English Translation in Ten Volumes*, vol. 10, Libri XXXVI-XXXVII, by D.E. Eichholz (Cambridge, 1971).

The Stained Glass Association of America, Reference and Technical Manual: A Comprehensive Guide to Stained Glass (Lee's Summit, 1992).

Stanley Smith, Cyril/ Hawthorne, John G., *"Mappae Clavicula,* A Little Key to the World of Medieval Techniques, An annotated translation based on a collection of the Selestat and Phillipps-Corning manuscripts, with reproductions of the two manuscripts," *Transactions of the American Philosophical Society*, vol. 64/4 (July 1974).

Whall, Christopher W., *Stained Glass Work: A Textbook for Students and Workers in Glass* (repr. London, 1920; orig. publ. in New York, 1905)

EXHIBITION CHECKLIST

I. Glass Panels in Exhibition

1 Artist unknown
Traditional Floral Patterned Window, 1880–1930
Collection Conrad Schmitt Studios, New Berlin, WI
28½ x 27 inches

2 Tiffany Glass & Decorating Company
Border Section from *Christ Blessing*, 1898
From Collegiate Church, New York, NY
Rohlf's Stained & Leaded Glass
45¼ x 13¼ inches

3 Louis Comfort Tiffany (1848-1933)
Fabrication Tiffany Studios, Corona, NY
Young Joseph, c. 1900
69¾ x 42¼ inches (framed)
The Corning Museum of Glass, 64.4.80, Gift of Dr. Robert Koch

4 The Munich Studio (1901–1938), Chicago, IL
Angel, c. 1910
57¾ x 23¾ inches
Collection Conrad Schmitt Studios, New Berlin, WI

5 Artist unknown
Border with Menorah, c. 1910
58¼ x 11 inches
Collection Conrad Schmitt Studios, New Berlin, WI

6 Thomas Augustin O'Shaughnessy (1870–1956)
For the Glory of God, after 1912
Old St. Patrick's Church, Chicago, IL
16¾ x 26⅛ inches
Collection Conrad Schmitt Studios, New Berlin, WI

7 Thomas Augustin O'Shaughnessy (1870–1956)
For the Love of Mankind, after 1912
Old St. Patrick's Church, Chicago, IL
16¾ x 26⅛ inches
Collection Conrad Schmitt Studios, New Berlin, WI

8 Artist unknown
Gothic Revival Patterned Window, 1930s
36 x 23 inches
Collection Conrad Schmitt Studios, New Berlin, WI

9 *Stylized Plant Border* (section), 1930s
26 x 10¼ inches
Collection Conrad Schmitt Studios, New Berlin, WI

10 Artist unknown
Wheat and Grapes, 1930s
23 x 20 inches
Collection Conrad Schmitt Studios, New Berlin, WI

11 Artist unknown
Opalescent "Prairie Style" Border, c. 1910–20
51½ x 14 inches
Collection Gaytee Stained Glass, Minneapolis, MN

12 Charles J. Connick (1875–1945)
Coronation of the Virgin (detail), late 1920s
39⅛ inches diameter
Charles J. Connick Collection, Fine Arts Department, Boston Public Library, Boston, MA

13 Artist unknown
Thistle Border, 1930s
29⅝ x 11¼ inches
Collection Gaytee Stained Glass, Minneapolis, MN

14 Weston and Leighton
Bible Window, 1943
Cathedral of the Holy Spirit, Bismarck, ND
29⅝ x 29⅝ x 1⅜
Collection Gaytee Stained Glass, Minneapolis, MN

15 Katharine Lamb Tait (1895–1981)
Fabricated by J & R Lamb Studios
My Covenant of Peace I Give to You, late 1940s
36⅜ x 20⅜ inches
Corning Museum of Glass, 91.4.96, Gift of Donald Samick

16 Artist unknown
St. George, 1950s?
54 x 21½ inches
Collection Franklin Art Glass, Columbus, OH

17 Artist unknown
Christ in the Garden of Gethsemane, 1950s?
50 x 18⅞ inches
Collection Franklin Art Glass, Columbus, OH

18 Robert Sowers (1923–1990)
Red One, 1952
16⅝ x 17¼ inches (framed)
Corning Museum of Glass, 92.2.6, Gift of Judi Jordan Sowers

19 Helen Carew Hickman (1925–)
Pietà, 1952
33¼ x 24⅜ inches
Corning Museum of Glass, 93.4.78, Gift of the artist

20 Fabricated by Conrad Schmitt Studios
Face of the Virgin and Infant Christ, 1960s?
16¾ x 10¼ inches
Collection Conrad Schmitt Studios, New Berlin, WI

21 Carl Huneke (1898-1972)
Fabricated by Century Stained Glass Studio, San Francisco, CA
Virgin and Child, 1961
43½ x 15 1/4 inches
Collection Terry Blaine

22 Hendrik van de Burgt
Fabricated by J & R Lamb Studios
The Sower, 1964
50¾ x 22½ inches
Collection Donald Samick, J & R Lamb Studios

23 Hendrik van de Burgt
Fabricated by J. & R. Lamb
Studios
Synagogue Window, 1970
58⅛ x 20⅛ inches
Collection Donald Samick,
J & R Lamb Studios

24 Robert Kehlmann
(1942–)
Entombment, Station 14,
1982
32¼ x 24¼ inches
Corning Museum of Glass,
83.4.1902

25 Sylvia Nicolas (1928–)
St. John the Evangelist,
1990s
28⅞ x 18 inches
Collection of the artist

26 Saara Gallin (1930–)
Mezuzah, 1999
36 inches diameter
Collection of the artist

27 Johannes Schreiter
(1930–)
Model window panels,
2001
Grunewaldkirche, Berlin
56 x 48 inches
Collection Derix Glasstudios, Taunusstein, Germany

28 Mary Clerkin Higgins
(1954–)
In the Beginning, 2002
33½ x 33⁹⁄₁₆ inches
Collection of the artist

29 J. Kenneth Leap (1964-)
Fabrication Assistance by
Derix Glasstudios,
Taunusstein, Germany
Peaceable Kingdom, 2002
57⅞ x 25 inches
Collection of the artist

II. Focus Artists

DOUGLAS HANSEN (1949–)

30 *IHS Window*, 1996
Wooden Model for Mold
Ignatius Chapel
Seattle University, Seattle,
WA
26½ x 42½ inches
Collection of the artist

31 *IHS Window*, 1996
Ignatius Chapel
Seattle University, Seattle,
WA
25½ x 41½ inches
Collection of the artist

STEPHEN KNAPP (1947–)

32 *Quattuordecim*, 2002
Lightpainting, dichroic
glass
10 x 16 feet
Collection of the artist

33 *Passages and Promises*,
2002
Float glass painting
35 x 77 inches
Collection of the artist

34 *Untitled*
Fused, kiln-formed glass
relief panel
40 x 80 inches
Collection of the artist

LINDA LICHTMAN (1941–)

35 Fabricted by Derix,
Taunusstein, Germany
Quercus Alba, 2002
20¼ x 22¼ inches
Collection of the artist

ELLEN MANDELBAUM (1938–)

36 Fabricated by Rohlf's
Stained & Leaded Glass
Mystic Rose Window, 2001
Marian Woods, Hartsdale,
NY
37½ x 54⅛ inches
Collection of the artist

ELLEN MIRET (1954–)

37 Fabricated by Rohlfs'
Stained & Leaded Glass
Stained glass panel
Ascension Mausoleum,
Monsey, NY
50 x 30 inches
Collection of the artist

DAVID WILSON (1941–)

38 Glass panel, 2002
Rehm Library, Center for
Religion, Ethics and
Culture, College of the
Holy Cross, Worcester, MA
52⁹⁄₁₆ x 40¼ inches
Collection of the artist

39 Glass panel, 2002
For the Spirit of Christ
Catholic Church,
Arvada, CO
31⅝ x 26¼ inches
Collection of the artist

III. Glass Process Material

*In addition to the lenders
of the panels on display
we would like to thank the
following artists for lending us various materials,
tools, sketches, and drawings, photographs, models,
and blueprints:*

Douglas Hansen
Stephen Knapp
Linda Lichtman
Ellen Mandelbaum
Ellen Miret
David Wilson

*Furthermore we are
grateful to:*

Derix Glasstudios,
Taunusstein, Germany
Glashütte Lamberts,
Waldsassen, Germany
Bendheim, Passaic, NJ
Kokomo Opalescent Glass,
Kokomo, IN
Uroboros Glass Studios,
Portland, OR
The St. Ann Center for
Restoration and the Arts,
Brooklyn, NY

*for generously lending
us process material
and assorted glasses
on display.*

PHOTOGRAPHIC ACKNOWLEDGEMENTS

Cover art
Figures **18, 20, 23, 27, 31, 32, 36, 38, 40, 48**
(all details)

Chapter 1: Stained Glass Considered: A Past Century and Today

Opening image, *Red One*, 1952 © The Corning Museum f Glass, 92.2.6, Gift of Judi Jordan Sowers

1 Charles J. Connick Collection, Fine Arts Department, Boston Public Library; Reproduced courtesy of the Trustees of the Boston Public Library

2 © The Corning Museum of Glass, 92.2.6, Gift of Judi Jordan Sowers

3 Photograph: Albinas Elskus

4–10 Photograph: Virginia Raguin

11 © Wadsworth Atheneum, Hartford. Gift of Susan Morse Hilles

12 Photograph © 2002, American Bible Society/ David Singer

13 Photograph © 2002, American Bible Society/ David Singer

14 © Warchol Photography

Chapter 2: The Opalescent Era: The New Century Begins

Opening image, see figure **19** (detail)

15 © The Corning Museum of Glass, 64.4.80, Gift of Dr. Robert Koch

16 The Metropolitan Museum of Art, Gift of George F. Baker, 1916. (16.95) Photograph © 1981, The Metropolitan Museum of Art

17 Photograph: Virginia Raguin

18 Photograph: Peter Rohlf

19 Brooklyn Museum of Art. Gift of Irving T. Bush in memory of his parents, Rufus T. and Sarah M. Bush (29.1082)/ Photograph: Scott Hyde

Chapter 3: Art Nouveau, Arts and Crafts, and Art Deco

Opening image, see figure **31** (detail)

20–24 Photograph: Virginia Raguin

25 Photograph: Conrad Schmitt Studios

26 Photograph: James Sturm

27, 28 Photograph: Conrad Schmitt Studios

29, 30 John Salisbury, Gaytee Stained Glass, Minneapolis, MN Photograph © 2002, The American Bible Society/Gina Fuentes Walker

31 © Art Resource, NY

32 John Salisbury, Gaytee Stained Glass, Minneapolis, MN Photograph © 2002, American Bible Society/ Gina Fuentes Walker

33 Photograph: Virginia Raguin

Chapter 4: Historical References: Gothic Revival and Beyond

Opening image, see figure **37** (detail)

34 Photograph: Erich Lessing / Art Resource, NY

35 Photograph: Virginia Raguin

36 Photograph: Conrad Schmitt Studios

37 Photograph: Conrad Schmitt Studios

38, 39 Reproduced courtesy of the Trustees of the Boston Public Library

40 Photograph: Virginia Raguin

41, 42 Photograph: Conrad Schmitt Studios

43, 44 Franklin Art Glass Studios Inc.; Fine Stained glass since 1924 Photograph © 2002, American Bible Society/ Gina Fuentes Walker

Chapter 5: The Last Fifty Years

Opening image, see figure **66** (detail)

45 Photograph: Derix Glasstudios, Taunusstein, Germany

46 Museum of Fine Arts, Boston; Gift of Barbara W. McCue and Gerald M. McCue; 1998.576 © 2002, Museum of Fine Arts, Boston

47 © Nicolas Sapieha/Art Resource © 2002 Kate Rothko-Prizel & Christopher Rothko/Artists Rights Society, New York

48 Photograph: Terry Blaine

49 Photograph: Historic Hudson Valley

50 Photograph: Arthur Stern

51 © The Corning Museum of Glass, 91.4.96, Gift of Donald Samick

52 Loan by Donald Samick, J & R Lamb Studios Photograph © 2002, American Bible Society/ Gina Fuentes Walker

53 Photo courtesy Benoit Gilsoul

54 © The Corning Museum of Glass, 92.2.6, Gift of Judi Jordan Sowers

55 © The Corning Museum of Glass, 93.4.78, Gift of Helen Carew Hickman

56 Photograph: Albinas Elskus

57 Photograph: Wilmark Studios

58 Photograph: Sylvia Nicolas

59 Photograph: Rohlf's Stained & Leaded Glass

60 Photograph: Saara Gallin

61 Photograph: Charles Z. Lawrence

62 © The Corning Museum of Glass, 83.4.1902

63 Photograph: Ed Carpenter and Edwardo Calderone

64 © James Carpenter Design, 1994

65 Photograph: Mark Eric Gulsrud

66 Photograph: Mary Clerkin Higgins

67 Photograph: Peter Groesbeck

Chapter 6: Stained Glass Window Fabrication

Opening image, see figures **68, 79** (details)

68 Courtesy Robert H. Brill, Corning Museum of Glass, Corning, NY

69 Courtesy Kokomo Opalescent Glass, Kokomo, IN Photograph © 2002, American Bible Society/ Gina Fuentes Walker

70–77 Photo courtesy Glashütte Lamberts, Waldsassen, Germany

78–81 Photo courtesy Kokomo Opalescent Glass, Kokomo, IN

82–87 Courtesy Uroboros Glass Studios, Portland, OR Photograph © 2002, American Bible Society/ Gina Fuentes Walker

88, 89 Courtesy Derix Glasstudios, Taunusstein, Germany Photograph © 2002, American Bible Society/ Gina Fuentes Walker

90 Photograph: David Fraser

91–93 Courtesy Derix Glasstudios, Taunusstein, Germany Photograph © 2002, American Bible Society/ Gina Fuentes Walker

Chapter 7: Focus Artists

Opening image, see figures **95, 96, 98, 191, 104, 108, 110** (details)

94, 95 Photograph: Douglas Hansen

96, 97 © Warchol Photography

98–100 Photograph: Stephen Knapp

101–103 Photograph: John Horner

104–106 Photograph: Ellen Mandelbaum

107–109 Photograph: Rohlf's Stained & Leaded Glass

110 Photograph: David Wilson

111, 112 Photograph: Virgina Raguin